Rudrangshu Mukherjee is a historian and journalist. Currently running the editorial pages of *The Telegraph*, he has held various academic posts and taught, among others at Calcutta, Princeton and Manchester universities. He is the author of several books, most recently *Mangal Pandey: Brave Martyr or Accidental Hero, India Then and Now, Awadh in Revolt, 1857-58: A Study of Popular Resistance* and *Spectre of Violence: The 1857 Kanpur Massacres* and is the editor of *The Penguin Gandhi Reader* and *Great Speeches of Modern India*. Rudrangshu Mukherjee lives in Kolkata.

Pramod Kapoor is a collector of historical records and photographs and a publisher by profession. The photographs for this book were lovingly collected over a long period of time from all over the world.

DATELINE 1857

Revolt against the Raj

ISBN: 978-81-7436-470-8

M-75 Greater Kailash II Market
New Delhi 110 048, India
Ph: ++91-11-29212782, 29210886;
Fax: ++91-11-29217185
E-mail: roli@vsnl.com
Website: rolibooks.com

Editor: Neelam Narula
Design: Mukesh Singh
Layout: Naresh Mondal
Production: Naresh Nigam, Kumar Raman

Printed and bound at Gopsons Paper Ltd. Noida, India.

Photo Credits:

Getty Images: Pg. 44, 46, 47, 48, 52, 56-57, 58-59, 60-61, 62-63, 64-65, 66, 69 (top), 69 (bottom), 70 (top), 71, 72-73, 75, 78 (top), 78 (bottom), 79, 84, 85, 86-87, 90, 91, 92-93, 94-95, 96-97, 98-99, 100, 101, 102 (top), 102 (bottom), 104, 105, 106-107, 108-109, 110-111, 112-113, 116, 117 (top), 117 (bottom), 119, 120, 124-125, 126-127, 128 (bottom), 129, Gatefold picture.

Corbis: Pg. 76-77, 80, 128 (top)

British Library: 67, 68, 70 (bottom), 74, 88, 89, 103 (top), 103 (bottom), 114-115, 118, 130 (top), 130 (bottom), 136

Public Records Office, Kew, London: Pg. 131, 132, 133, 134, 135

Maps: Tanmoy Chakraborty

DATELINE 1857
Revolt against the Raj

Text: Rudrangshu Mukherjee
Photo Research and Editing: Pramod Kapoor

Lustre Press
Roli Books

ACKNOWLEDGEMENTS

Around thirty years ago, Barun De took me under his wing and encouraged me to think and write about the revolt of 1857. I have learnt from him and others and it is my privilege to acknowledge here some of those intellectual debts. I had the good fortune to discuss the rebellion with Eric Stokes, and before his untimely death he read and approved of my first work on the subject. In Oxford, John Dunbabin and Tapan Raychaudhuri read my work and forced me to write clearly and precisely. In Calcutta, I have learnt from Asok Sen and Partha Chatterjee more than they would ever care to admit. At different times, Christopher Hill, Lawrence Stone and E.P. Thompson read my work and encouraged me in my quest to understand the rebellion. It was a privilege to have known these three past masters and to have received their affection.
'*Think where man's glory most begins and ends/ And say my glory was I had such friends.*'

I am blessed with the most wonderful set of colleagues in the editorial department of *The Telegraph*: to Aveek Sen, Bhaswati Chakravorty, Chirosree Basu, Sreyashi Dastidar and Uddalok Mukherjee – a very big thank you. Aveek Sarkar pushes me continuously to think clearly and write in a manner that is accessible to a world beyond the groves of academia. I am grateful to him for keeping me on my toes. There are others without whose love and affection writing would be impossible, life inconceivable. They shall remain unnamed: this is not the place for private words.

The credit for the photographs belongs to Pramod Kapoor while nobody save myself is responsible for the errors that remain in the book.

RUDRANGSHU MUKHERJEE
Kolkata, January 2008

In memory

of

S. Gopal

and

Ashin Das Gupta

'The Guide and I entered by that hidden road,
to return into the bright world; and without
caring for any rest, we mounted up, he first and
I second, so far that I distinguished through a
round opening the beauteous things which Heaven
bears; and thence we issued out again to see the Stars.'
Dante, *Inferno*, canto xxxiv

CONTENTS

AFGHANISTAN
PAKISTAN
NEPAL
SRI LANKA
JAMMU & KASHMIR
Srinagar
Jammu
Pathankot
HIMACHAL PRADESH
Lahore
Amritsar
Ludhiana
Shimla
Chandigarh
PUNJAB
Dehradun
Ambala
HARYANA
Meerut
Moradabad
Delhi
UNITED PROVINCES OF AWADH
Bulandshahr
Aligarh
Bareilly
Bahraich
Gonda
Faizabad
Bikaner
Jaisalmer
RAJASTHAN
Jaipur
Agra
Lucknow
Kanpur
Azamgarh
Jodhpur
Gwalior
Allahabad
Jhansi
Mhow
Benares
Patna
Kota
Udaipur
MADHYA PRADESH
Sagar
Bhuj
GUJARAT
Gandhinagar
Kandla
Ahmedabad
Bhopal
Jabalpur
Ranchi
Rajkot
Indore
Porbandar
Vadodara
Surat
CHHATTISGARH
Nagpur
Raipur
ORISSA
Diu
Silvassa
Cuttack
MAHARASHTRA
MUMBAI
Pune
Sholapur
Hyderabad
Vishakapatnam
Kakinada
Vijayawada
Panaji
GOA
KARNATAKA
ANDHRA PRADESH
Mangaluru
CHENNAI
Bangalore
Pondicherry (Puducherry)
Kozhikode
Coimbatore
TAMIL NADU
Tiruchirapalli
Kavarati
Kochi
Madurai
KERALA
Tuticorin
Thiruvananthapuram
2
3
4
5
6

STORM CENTRES OF THE UPRISING

1. Barrackpore
2. Meerut
3. Delhi
4. Lucknow
5. Kanpur
6. Jhansi

OTHER CENTRES

- Ambala
- Bareilly
- Allahabad
- Benares
- Mhow
- Gonda
- Azamgarh
- Bahraich
- Bulandshahr
- Moradabad
- Faizabad
- Aligarh
- Sagar
- Agra
- Lahore

DATELINE

1857

22 January
The sepoys at DumDum become uneasy about the new cartridges

January-March
Unrest among the sepoys on the greased cartridge question; outbreaks at Berhampore and Barrackpore. The chapaties pass from village to village.

24 April
Meerut. 3rd Bengal Light Cavalry; rebellious conduct followed by court-martial

10 May
Meerut. 3rd Light Cavalry, 11th N.I. revolt. Rebels kill officers and other Europeans and burn bungalows, set off for Delhi.

11 May
Rebels arrive Delhi; proclaim Bahadur Shah Zafar as Emperor, murder Europeans. Delhi troops 5th Light Fd Battery Foot Artillery, 3rd Bn 2nd Company, 38th N.I. and 54th N.I. all revolt. Magazine blown up by Lieutenant Willoughby and handful of British. European survivors retreat first to Flagstaff Tower, and then Karnal. Delhi and surrounding area in the control of the rebels.

20 May
At Aligarh a portion of the 9th N.I revolt, followed at Mainpuri and Bulandshahr on the 22nd and Etawa on 23rd, by the remainder of the regiment.

30 May
Revolt at Lucknow, 7th Light Cavalry, and (portions of) the 13th N.I., 48th N.I., and 71st N.I. Outbreak at Mathura; rebels march to Delhi. Battle of the Hindun River.

31 May
Bareilly, 18th N.I., 68th N.I., 15th Light Fd Battery, and 8th Irreg. Cavalry revolt. Khan Bahadur Khan, a government pensioner takes the lead, and is proclaimed ruler under the King of Delhi. At Shahjahanpur the 28th N.I. revolts and attacks the Christians. At Agra the native regiments are disarmed; Moradabad in open revolt.

1 June
At Moradabad the 29th N.I. revolts. Sepoys at Mathura shoot officers and march for Delhi. Outbreak at Budaon.

2 June
5th N.I. revolts at Saharanpur.

3 June
At Neemuch the entire force revolts viz. 1st Light Cavalry, 4th Troop 1st Brigade horse artillery, 15th Light Fd Battery, 72nd N.I. At Azamgarh the 17th N.I. revolts. At Sitapur the 41st N.I. revolts with particular ferocity against the European officers and civilians. Abbas Ali proclaims himself ruler in Moradabad.

4 June
Partial revolt at Benares by 37th N.I. General Neill arrives and disarms some troops. Revolt at Kanpur by 2nd Light cavalry, 1st N.I., 74th N.I., and 56th N.I. First group of Europeans leaves Fatehgarh.

5 June
53rd N.I. joins the revolt at Kanpur, General Wheeler calls all Europens and Christians into his 'entrenchments'.

6 June
Siege of Wheeler's entrenchment at Kanpur begins. Nana Sahib joins the rebels and is proclaimed Peshwa, 12th N.I. at Jhansi revolt, and massacre of the Europeans follows; 4th Company 9th Bn Artillery at Azamgarh revolt; at Allahabad (part) 6th N.I. revolt. Nawab of Rampur visits Moradabad to take charge.

8 June
The Battle of Badli-ki-Serai in Delhi; British troops occupy the Ridge, and the 'siege' of Delhi begins. At Phillour the 3rd N.I. revolt. At Faizabad the 22nd N.I., and the 13th Lt Fd Battery 5th Bn 2nd company revolt.

11 June
Brigadier General James Neill arrives at Allahabad. Jhansi rebels leave for Delhi.

12 June
Massacre by Nana Sahib of 130 European fugitives from Fatehgarh at Bithur.

15 June
Wajid Ali Shah, ex-King of Awadh and chief councillors imprisoned in Fort William in Calcutta. Bareilly Brigade reaches Moradabad enroute for Delhi.

16 June
Maulvi Liaqat Ali flies from Allahabad. Nawab's rule proclaimed at Fatehgarh.

18 June
At Fatehgarh the 10th N.I. (previously loyal) eventually break into revolt. Mewati and Pathan villages in Allahabad district attacked and destroyed by the British.

25 June
At Kanpur the Nana Sahib offers terms to Wheeler in the entrenchment. Revolt at Malthone. Sack of Deoli.

27 June
Massacre at Satichaura Ghat, Kanpur.

28 June
Fatehgarh Fort besieged by rebels. Nagode gaol broken into.

30 June
British defeated at Chinhat; Lucknow Residency surrounded and besieged. Bulandshahr captured by Walidad Khan.

2 July
Bakht Khan arrives at Delhi with the Bareilly Brigade. Pearson's Battery and Cavalry revolt at Agra.

4 July
Massacre at Rampore on Ganges of Europen fugitives from Fatehgarh/Farrukhabad. Sir Henry Lawrence, dies in the Lucknow Residency.

7 July
General Havelock leaves Allahabad en route for Kanpur.

12 July
Fatehpur occupied by Havelock.

15 July
Action at Anog (Renaud killed), and at Pandu Nadi. 'Massacre of the Ladies' i.e. Bibighur massacre at Kanpur.

16 July
Nana Sahib defeated by Havelock at Fatehpur, and First Battle of Kanpur. Nana Sahib orders all Bengali Babus to be apprehended.

17 July
Havelock enters Kanpur and the Nana Sahib retreats to Bithur.

25 July
The Danapur Brigade revolt, i.e. the 7th N.I., 8th N.I., 40th N.I.

27 July
Siege of Arrah House begins.

28 July
'Parade Ground Massacre' at Farruckhabad (Fatehgarh). Azimgarh evacuated by the British.

29 July
Havelock defeats rebels at Unnao.

31 July
The large rebel force from Mhow and Indore arrives at Gwalior, leaving Scindia helpless to prevent their onward march towards Agra.

3 August
Arrah House relieved by Major Eyre.

5 August
Havelock defeats the rebels at Bashiratganj. Kunwar Singh reported to have proclaimed himself 'King of Shahbad'.

8 August
Khan Bahadur Khan's forces from Bareilly reported as advancing to attack Nainital. Rebels' gunpowder factory in Delhi blown up.

11 August
Eyre burns Kunwar Singh's palace at Jagdishpur.

12 August
Havelock defeats Awadh rebels in the third battle of Bashiratganj.

13 August
Havelock defeats Awadh rebels in the third battle of Bashiratganj.

14 August
Movable Column under John Nicholson arrives at Delhi. Kunwar Singh arrives at Sassaram.

16 August
Havelock defeats the forces of Nana Sahib at Bithur.

17 August
Sir Colin Campbell takes over duties as British Commander-in-Chief.

19 August
At Ferozepur the 10th Light Cavalry revolt. Kunwar Singh at Akbarpur. Amar Singh threatens to burn Dehri.

20 August
Kunwar Singh at Rohtasgarh.

25 August
Firoz Shah, Shahzada, placed on the musnud at Mandsaur.

26 August
Outbreak at Mandsaur

29 August
At Peshawar the disarmed 51st N.I. revolt, and many are slaughtered. Kunwar Singh arrives at Ramgarh, and plunders Ghorawal.

7 September
Kunwar Singh closes road to Rewa.

8 September
Kunwar Singh marches through Mirzapur, and reported to have arrived in Rewa. Jung Bahadur's Gurkhas arrive at Jaunpur.

14 September
British begin the assault on Delhi.

19 September
Havelock and Outram set out from Kanpur for Lucknow.

20 September
After fierce fighting Delhi finally conquered by the British.

21 September
Captain Hodson claims to have captured the King of Delhi, Bahadur Shah Zafar at Humayun's Tomb.

22 September
Hodson murders the Mughal Princes.

25 September
Lucknow Residency 'relieved' by Havelock. Neill and Tytler killed, together with 600 other British casualties.

29 September
Kunwar Singh reaches Banda. Said to be accompanied by 1,800 of Danapore rebels.

5 October
Walidad Khan reaches Bareilly with 500 followers. Greathed's Column meets opposition at Aligarh.

8 October
Nawab of Banda attacks fortress of Ajaigarh.

13 October
Two Shahzadas, Mirza Bakhtawar Shah and Mirza Mendu, sons of the King of Delhi, tried by the British and shot beside the Jumna.

15 October
Gwalior Contingent joins the rebels. Outbreak at Kotah.

19 October
Kunwar Singh with the 40th BNI reaches Kalpi via Banda.

29 October
Tatya Tope with Gwalior Contingent arrives at Jalaun.

7 November
Gwalior Contingent and 40th BNI (with Kunwar Singh) join up and begin advance on Kanpur.

17 November
Sir Colin Campbell relieves and evacuates the Lucknow Residency, leaving Outram at the Alambagh; rebels see his withdrawal from Awadh as a great victory.

24 November
Havelock dies of dysentery; buried in the Alambagh.

27 November
Gwalior Contingent attacks Nawabganj (Kanpur) and forces the British to retire into entrenchments.

3 December
Campbell dispatches all the ladies and sick, ex Lucknow Residency, to Allahabad.

6 December
Campbell defeats Tatya Tope in the third battle of Kanpur.

1858

6 January
Campbell re-occupies Fatehgarh. Sir Hugh Rose begins Central India campaign.

7 January
Trial of Bahadur Shah Zafar begins in Red Fort Delhi. (Ends March 9th)

14 January
Rani of Jhansi issues a proclamation against the British – 'Victory of Religion'.

23 January
Rebels mustering again at Kalpi.

28 January
Fortress of Rahatgarh taken by Rose.

3 February
Sir Hugh Rose relieves Sagar.

5 February
Action at Ayodhya between rebels and Jung Bahadur's Gurkhas.

7 February
General Whitlock with Madras troops arrives Jabalpur.

10 February
Nana Sahib at Naubatganj.

12 February
Kunwar Singh reported to be arriving at Ayodhya.

18 February
Proclamation issued by Firoz Shah at Bareilly.

25 February
Nana Sahib reported to be at Kalpi.

1 March
Tehri troops beaten by Rani's forces. Charkhari captured.

2–21 March
Campbell retakes Lucknow; drives out the rebels led by the Maulvi of Faizabad and the Begum of Awadh. Lucknow stormed on 14th.

16 March
Nana Sahib reported to be at Shahjahanpur.

17 March
Brigadier Stuart takes Chanderi by storm. Battle of Atraulia, victory for Kunwar Singh.

18 March
Nawabs of Farrukhabad and Banda, Raja Tej Singh of Mainpuri, Khan Bahadur Khan of Bareilly, Walidad Khan specifically excluded from the benefit (i.e. free pardon etc.) of British Proclamation offering a reward of rupees one lakh to rebel betraying Nana Sahib.

21 March
Rose arrives at Jhansi.

22 March
Millman besieged in Azimgarh by Kunwar Singh.

23 March
Investment of Jhansi begins.

24 March
Explosion in Khan Bahadur Khan's gunpowder factory at Bareilly. Nana Sahib arrives at Bareilly.

26 March
Kunwar Singh occupies Azamgarh.

1 April
Battle of Betwa River. Rose defeats Tatya Tope.

3 April
Jhansi captured and sacked.

5 April
Jhansi fort taken by the British. Rani, with her step-son, reaches Kunch.

6 April
Lord Mark Kerr relieves Azimgarh.

15 April
General Walpole defeated at Royah; Brigadier Adrian Hope killed.

16 April
Kunwar Singh driven from Azamgarh by General Lugard.

17 April
Rao Sahib issues proclamation to Chiefs of Bundelkhand. Kunwar Singh attacked by Brigadier Douglas near Azmatgarh.

18 April
Battle of Banda.

21 April
Kunwar Singh crosses the Ganges at Sheopur Ghat and is mortally wounded while doing so.

22 April
Prince Firoz Shah reaches Moradabad.

23 April
Kunwar Singh defeats the British under Le Grand at Jagdishpur. Rose captures Kalpi.

24 April
Forces of Nawab of Rampur drive Firoz Shah from Moradabad.

26 April
Death of Kunwar Singh.

28 April
Rao Sahib encamped at Jalalpur to oppose Whitlock Gurkha army reaches Faizabad and Ayodhya.

3 May
Maulvi Ahmadullah Shah with large force comes from Mohammadi to Shahjahanpur.

6 May
Battle of Bareilly, included the famous change of the Ghazis of whom 133 were bayonettled. Bareilly taken but rebel leaders escaped.

8 May
Battle of Kunch, Rose defeats Tatya Tope.

10 May
General Lugard occupied Jagdishpur.

11 May
Amar Singh defeated by Corfield near Piru but manages to escape. Battle of Shahjahanpur.

13 May
Rebels menace British position and camp at Jagdishpur.

15 May
Rebel leaders including Nana Sahib, Khan Bahadur Khan and Maulvi Ahmadullah Shah all in vicinity of Shahjahanpur.

22 May
Battle of Kalpi, Rose captures the arsenal of Kalpi.

24 May
Second Battle of Shahjahanpur rebels defeated by Campbell and driven back to Mohammadi but followed up; British occupy Mohammadi.

25 May
Hamirpur occupied by the British.

1 June
Rani of Jhansi, Rao Sahib and Tatya Tope capture Gwalior. Nawab of Banda also present. Lushkar and Gwalior fort occupied. Madho Singh captured by Rose.

12 June
Battle of Nawabganj; Sir Hope Grant defeats 16,000 rebels in final decisive battle in Awadh. Amar Singh returns to Buxar. Khan Bahadur Khan attacks Shahjahanpur.

15 June
Maulvi Ahmadullah Shah attacks Pawayan, and is killed.

16 June
Battle of Morar. Raja of Pawayan brings head of Maulvi Ahmadullah Shah to the British at Shahjahanpur to claim the reward.

17 June
Battle of Kotah-ki-Serai; death of Rani of Jhansi.

19 June
Battle of Gwalior. City is occupied.

20 June
Gwalior Fort captured by Rose. Battle of Jaora-Alipur. Scindia returns to Gwalior.

5 July
Banpur raja surrenders to the British.

9 July
Tonk occupied by rebels; Firoz Shah reported to be with them.

10 July
Shahgarh raja surrenders. Rebel force reaches Rampur.

11 July
Ramnagar occupied by the rebels.

26 July
Pawayan and Shahjahanpur reported as 'seriously threatened' by Awadh rebels.

27 July
Force besieging Shahganj breaks up.

31 July
Sir Hope Grant relieves Raja Man Singh besieged by rebels.

1 November
Queen Victoria's Proclamation abolishing the rule of the Honourable East India Company in India and instituting her own.

12 November
Battle of Shankarpur, Beni Madho driven northwards, reported as joining up with Bala Rao.

25 November
Raja of Gonda defeated by Sir Patrick Grant, Gonda occupied.

5 December
Nana Sahib was reported as crossing the Ganges between Fatehgarh and Kanpur.

6 December
Firoz Shah and Walidad Khan reported at Aroul.

17 December
Firoz Shah's brief encounter with British force under Napier.

23 December
Bala Rao driven from Tulsipur and retreats into Nepal.

December
Bihar rebels finally dispersed.

1859

7 January
The rebellion in Awadh officially declared at an end.

9 January
Prince Firoz Shah cuts his way across Awadh and the Ganges; joins Tatya Tope temporarily.

29 January
Nawab of Farrukhabad arrives at Fatehgarh, under arrest.

28 March
Nana Sahib, Begum of Awadh reported to be at Butwal.

7 April
Khan Bahadur Khan, Begum of Awadh, Nana Sahib and Birjis Qadr reported to be in the fort of Niacote in Nepal.

8 April
Tatya Tope betrayed and captured.

18 April
Tatya Tope hanged.

20 April
Nana Sahib sends Ishtiharnama to Queen Victoria. Petition to the English from Bala Rao.

8 July
State of peace officially declared throughout India.

24 September
The death of the Nana Sahib reported.

December
Amar Singh captured in the Terai by Jung Bahadur's troops and handed over to the British.

9 December
Capture of Khan Bahadur Khan by Jung Bahadur reported.

17 December
Khan Bahadur Khan and Mammu Khan lodged in Lucknow Gaol.

1860

24 March
Khan Bahadur Khan of Bareilly hanged on the spot where he had raised the flag of revolt.

3 May
Jwala Prasad hanged at the Satichaura Ghat.

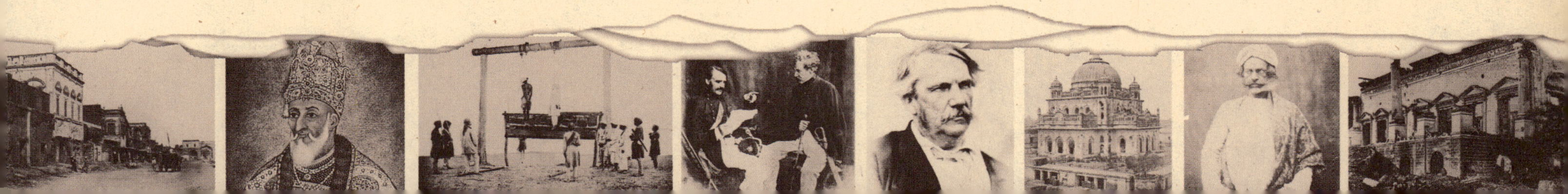

1857: The Great Uprising

A prophecy circulating in North India predicted that British rule would come to an end at the centenary of Plassey. Prophecies, rumours and fears that the British were bent on destroying a familiar way of life spurred men to action. The revolt brought together princes, big landholders, sepoys, peasants and ordinary people. Their many histories and diverse hopes came together as they fought to redeem their own past.

MEN AND OMENS

THE CANTONMENT OF BARRACKPORE, sixteen miles up river from Calcutta, was the military headquarters of the Presidency division of Bengal. There was located the country retreat of the Governor-General and stationed there was the largest body of Indian troops in eastern India. White inhabitants of Calcutta used Barrackpore as an escape from the noise and the pollution of the growing city. In the beginning of 1857 nobody could have predicted that from Barrackpore would come a signal that the loyalty of the sepoys could no longer be taken for granted by the rulers.

29 March in 1857 was a Sunday. But within the cantonment the usual calm of a Sunday afternoon was broken by a sepoy called Mangal Pandey who, probably under the influence of some intoxicating drug, was in a rage outside the quarter-guard. He was dressed in his regimental jacket but instead of his trousers he wore a *dhoti*; he was barefoot and carried with him a loaded musket. He called upon the bugler to sound the assembly, and to the other sepoys, he shouted, 'Come out, you *bhainchutes* [sisterfuckers], the Europeans are here! Why aren't you getting ready? It's our religion! From biting these cartridges we shall become infidels. Get ready! Turn out all of you! You have incited me to do this and now you *bhainchutes*, you will not follow me!'[1]

The commotion brought to the parade ground the adjutant, Lieutenant Baugh. Mangal Pandey opened fire and hit Baugh's horse. This grounded the lieutenant who jumped to his feet, shot at the sepoy, missed him and charged towards him. Behind him was Sergeant-Major Hewson. Mangal Pandey met them with his sabre drawn; he slashed at Baugh, cutting him on the shoulder and neck. Hewson was hit from behind by a sepoy wielding his musket. Both Baugh and Hewson would probably have been killed had it not been for Shaikh Paltu, a Muslim sepoy, who held back Mangal Pandey by gripping him around the waist. This enabled the two Englishmen to escape.

The next to appear was the commanding officer of the 34th Native Infantry (N.I.), Colonel S.G. Wheler. He ordered the guard to arrest Mangal Pandey and they refused. Expressing his helplessness, Wheler was to later testify before the court of inquiry that he 'felt it was useless going any further into the matter.' By the time the officer commanding the division, Major-General Hearsey, accompanied by his two sons, arrived, the situation seemed to have spun out of control. As Hearsey rode towards the sepoy, someone shouted, 'His musket is loaded.' To this, Hearsey retorted, 'Damn his musket.' When his elder son warned, 'Father, he is taking aim at you,' the General instructed him, 'If I fall John, rush upon him and put him to death.'

Hearsey rode up to the quarter-guard and shouted, waving his pistol at them, 'Listen to me. The first man who refuses to march when I give the word is a dead man. Quick march.' This time there was no disobedience and defiance. But as they approached, Mangal Pandey turned his musket towards his own chest and pulled the trigger with his toe. The attempt at suicide failed: the bullet only ripped apart the muscles of his chest, shoulder and neck.

At his trial, Mangal Pandey insisted that he had acted on his own and his defiance had not been part of a wider conspiracy. During his interrogation, he was repeatedly asked to give the names of those who, as he had said, had incited him. He refused and reiterated that he had acted on his own will. When asked if he had been intoxicated, he said, 'Yes, I have been taking *bhang* and opium of late. I was not aware at the time of what I was doing.' He added, 'I did not know who I wounded and who I did not. What more shall I say? I have nothing more to say. I have no evidence.' This was Mangal Pandey's plea in his own defence. He was condemned to death and was hanged on 8 April 1857.

The Mangal Pandey episode and the trial that followed have left historians with too many unanswered questions. It is difficult to accept the self-implicating statements that he made at his own trial. Even without advocating a conspiracy theory, there is the fact that no sepoy, save Shaikh Paltu, came forward to stop him or aid the British officers till General Hearsey arrived on the scene and threatened dire consequences. When the sergeant-major asked the *jemadar* (Indian officer with the rank equivalent of a lieutenant) at the quarter-guard why Mangal Pandey had not been arrested, he was told, 'What can I do? The *naick* has gone to the adjutant. The *havildar* has gone to the field officer. Am I to take him myself?' The apparent helplessness expressed by the *jemadar* could signify a number of things or all of them: his own tacit complicity, delaying tactics to get white officers, the intended targets on to the scene and his knowledge that Mangal Pandey had the support of numbers and it would not be easy to overpower him. That the British officers did not buy the plea of helplessness was proved when the *jemadar* was also condemned to death on 21 April.

That Mangal Pandey had tacit support cannot be ruled out. A large number of sepoys had gathered in the parade ground and they did not come forward to uphold authority and discipline. They may not have been ripe for an open mutiny but their collective inactivity displayed a certain proneness to defiance and disobedience, which can only be read as approval of Mangal Pandey's actions. When Hearsey chided them for failing to do their duty, they replied, 'He had loaded his musket.' Hearsey replied, 'What, are you afraid of a loaded musket?' and they were silent. It should not be forgotten that one unidentified sepoy knocked out Hewson with a blow from his musket. Whatever action there had been from the sepoys on that afternoon had been on the side of the rebel. Discipline had ultimately prevailed, but only just.

What are we then to make of Mangal Pandey's silence? Was he protecting his comrades? Do we read in his steadfast refusal to answer queries a statement of rebel solidarity?

When the 34th N.I., the regiment to which Mangal Pandey had belonged, was disbanded in April 1857, they threw their caps on the ground and trampled them before leaving the parade ground. Such gestures of disapproval would translate into hatred and violence in the cantonments across North India in the month of May. And Mangal Pandey's caste name would become among British troops the common pejorative term to describe a rebel sepoy.[2]

Mangal Pandey's warning about the cartridges offers a clue to what was making the sepoys restive in Barrackpore and other cantonments in North India. The standard weapon used by the sepoys had been the musket nicknamed Brown Bess. It was decided to replace this in the Indian and the British Army by an improved weapon with grooved bores like a rifle. The new rifle introduced in India in 1856 was seen, even by the sepoys, to be a more efficient firearm with greater reach. But in the sepoy lines, opinion in favour of this new 'Enfield' rifle (the gun was produced in Enfield) was short-lived. The new rifle could not be loaded without lubrication of the cartridge. And it was put out, by nobody knows who, that the cartridge, the end of which had to be bitten off by the sepoy, was greased with the fat of pigs and cows (Kaye: I: 488-89).

If the author of the rumour was unknown, its beginning could be traced to an incident in Dum Dum near Calcutta. In January 1857, a *lascar* (magazine-man) belonging to a low caste asked a Brahmin sepoy for a drink of water from the latter's *lotah* (a brass jug with a spout used for carrying water). The sepoy refused on the grounds of caste. The *lascar* retorted with the taunt that very soon there would be no distinction between high and low castes as new cartridges smeared with the fat of pigs and cows were being manufactured for general use in the army. The story about the new cartridges caught on and spread through the sepoy lines and was soon seen as part of a deliberate plot by the British to despoil the caste and religion of Indians. It sent shudders of fear among the sepoys and made them suspicious and defiant (Kaye: I: 490). Their emotions were displayed through destruction of government property; fire became the symbol of the sepoy's fear and anger. A few days after the incident in Dum Dum, the telegraph office in Barrackpore was burnt down. Night after night burning arrows were shot into the thatched roofs of officers' bungalows. Reports filtered through to the British of nocturnal meetings of sepoys where men with their faces hidden discussed excitedly about their future and their course of action (Kaye: I: 497). Had Mangal Pandey been a part of these discussions? Was he referring to these meetings when he spoke of incitement by his comrades?

If such questions are unanswerable on the basis of the available documents, the historical record is replete with references to the speed with which the rumours spread and the proportions they acquired. Somewhat like the *complot aristocratique* in revolutionary France, there spread along the sepoy lines of North India the fear of a plot to pollute the caste and religion of Indian soldiers through contamination. The alleged use of pig and cow fat – the one forbidden by Islam and the other by Hinduism – alarmed both Muslims and Hindus. From the fear of the greased cartridge, the suspicion extended to other items of daily use by the entire population. One officer from North India wrote:

> Government, it was said, had sent up cartloads and boatloads of bone-dust, which was to be mixed up with the flour and sweetmeats sold in the bazaar, whereby the whole population would lose their caste. The public mind became greatly excited. On one day at Sultanpoor, it was spread over the station that a boat had arrived at a certain ghaut on the river Goomtee laden with bone-dust, and the sepoys were hardly restrained from outbreak. A few days later at the station of Salone, two camels laden with ammunition, arrived at the house of Captain Thompson, the commandant. It was rumoured that the packages contained bone-dust and a panic spread through the station. Not only the sepoys in their lines, but the domestic servants about the officers' bungalows, and the villagers and zemindars attending court, hastily flung away, untasted, the food which they had cooked, and fasted for the day. At Lucknow, the rumours which were whispered about were perpetual, and the public mind was never allowed to rest. Now it was at one shop, the next day in another bazaar, that despatches of bone-dust had, it was asserted, been received. It was in vain that facts were opposed to this prevailing panic. (Gubbins: 86)

Salt, sugar, wheat, ghee and even water, it was believed, had been contaminated by the British in an attempt to make Hindus and Muslims lose their religion and then to convert them to Christianity. The plot aimed at all the classes and the British had ordered all the princes, nobles, landholders, merchants and cultivators of the land 'to feed together upon English bread' (Kaye: I: 568). Henry Lawrence, the chief commissioner of Awadh, was 'startled by the dogged persistence' of a *jemadar* in the Awadh artillery – a man of 'excellent character,' according to Lawrence – 'in the belief that for ten years past Government had been engaged in measures for the forcible or rather fraudulent conversion of all natives.'[3] Rumours about pollution circulated and spread alarm. In Vellore, in July 1806, when the sepoys had mutinied, similar rumours about pollution and conversion had excited the sepoys (Kaye: I: 220-252). No amount of persuasion by the rulers convinced the sepoys that conversion was not one of the aims of the sahibs.

Untraceable in their origin and unverifiable in their import, the rumours moved in a powerful current touching on issues that were profoundly close to indigenous sentiments. In the popular mind, the rumours came to be linked with the prophecy prevalent in 1857 that British rule would come to an end at the centenary of the battle of Plassey (1757) (Kaye: I: 484-86). A loyal sepoy, Sitaram, in his recollections, a rare statement in the context of 1857, wrote, 'Our learned men ... told us that the Company's rule would come to an end in 1857, since this was one hundred years after the Company's first great battle' (Sitaram: 173). The nature of this prediction and the way it was recollected and retold gave to it the character of what Keith Thomas in his study of popular culture and popular beliefs in sixteenth and seventeenth century England described as 'ancient prophecies': it was attributed most of the time to some mythical or historical personage ('our learned men', Sitaram said, with veneration) and the prophecy was invariably very old (Thomas: 461-62). For 1857, Kaye, whose eyes hardly ever missed anything of significance concerning the uprising of 1857, recorded an instance in which the prophecy about the end of British rule in 1857 had been made 1000 years ago, i.e., even before the British had set eyes on India (Kaye: I: 485n).

The circulation of prophecies and rumours has a tendency to alarm authorities for there is in history an association of rebellion with such circulation. Thomas has shown how in early modern England uprisings in the North and East Ridings of Yorkshire were stimulated by prophecy; the peasants who followed Robert Kett in Norfolk were similarly inspired by a prophecy. The authorities described the prophecies as 'the very foundation of all rebellion' (Thomas: 478-79). But rumours and prophecies had more to them than the alarm they spread among those who had most to lose in a popular uprising. Rumours, as Ranajit Guha has pointed out in his study of peasant insurgencies, were 'the *universal* and *necessary* carrier of insurgency in any pre-industrial and pre-literate society.' Rumours are by definition authorless and spread by word of mouth. They always seize upon the issue of the day; their circulation is a product of and an addition to prevailing social tension. They have a functional immediacy. In times of insurgency, they act as a trigger as well as a mobilizer. They become an instrument of rebel transmission and help in the movement of the message of rebellion. Guha drew attention to another important aspect of rumours and their circulation. Rumours have embedded in them a socializing aspect. They originate and circulate in places where people assemble in large numbers. Kaye noted this when he described the rumours of 1857 as 'the lies of the bazaar' (Kaye: I: 492).

Rumours in 1857 – greased cartridges, forcible conversion to Christianity by mixing bone-dust with flour, the end of the Company's rule at the centenary of Plassey, the disarming of native regiments – touched profoundly on indigenous sentiments and merged together to become one gigantic rumour. In the bazaars and in the sepoy lines, inaccessible to the British, the rumours moved through a 'comradeship response'. This gave the rumours speed: Kaye commented that the swiftness with which the rumours moved from one station to another was 'almost electric' (Kaye: I: 491). In the context of rumours in 1857, Kaye noted the vernacular saying, 'It is in the air', and wrote: 'We cannot trace the progress of these evil tidings ... It often happened that an uneasy feeling – an impression that something had happened, though they could not discern the shape thereof – pervaded men's minds, in obscure anticipation of the news travelling towards them in all its tangible proportions' (Kaye: I: 491-92). A rumour cannot be pinned down, as Kaye noted. This is what makes rumours, according to Guha, 'a mobile and explosive agent of insurgency'. Rumours, because they are anonymous and unverifiable are open: they are transitive and free; their circulation is unpremeditated and therefore prone to improvisation.[4] Rumours in 1857 created alarm about the government's intentions about polluting people's caste and religion, and pushed men to act.

If rumours foxed the British, the circulation of *chapattis* completely mystified them. The phenomenon of *chapattis* – small flat pieces of leavened bread, the staple of North India – has become the most talked about aspect of the year 1857 ever since it was first noticed in February-March of that year. The officer who was among the first to notice the occurrence left a vivid account:

> ... a signal has passed through numbers of the villages of this district, the purport of which has not yet transpired. The Chowkeydars [watchmen] of the villages bordering on those belonging to Mutra have received small baked cakes of atta with orders to distribute them generally through this district. A Chowkeydar, upon receiving one of these cakes, has had five or six more prepared, and thus they have passed from village to village; so quickly has the order been executed that village after village has been served with this notice. (Quoted in Kaye: I: 632)

Another report from around the same time but from the area around Agra also noted the same details:

> In the commencement of 1857, while marching through the Mynpoory district, my attention was drawn by Zemindars in villages adjoining the road to a mysterious distribution of chupattees (or small wheaten cakes), with astonishing rapidity through the country. The bearers knew apparently no more than those from whom they last received the cakes what the purport of the injunction was which directed the preparation of five cakes to be carried on to the villages in advance. "They would be called for," it was stated, and in this way chupattees or their counterparts travelled often over 160 or 200 miles in a night .... All endeavours failed to discover any explanation of this mysterious movement, [but] I have reason to believe that it had some bearing upon the Hindu prophecy limiting British rule to a centenary of years.[5]

It is significant that as soon as the phenomenon was first noticed it was read as a signal in one case and in another it was directly linked to the prophecy about the end of British rule one hundred years after the battle of Plassey. This set the trend for the way the circulation of *chapattis* was interpreted in the post-mortem of the uprising. British officers admitted that they did not know exactly what the *chapattis* had denoted but they were convinced that it was linked to the rebellion that followed their circulation. One officer wrote, 'The natives generally may have viewed this sign-manual flying through their villages ... as a forerunner of some universal popular outbreak.'[6] Another officer saw the mystery of the chapatti solved by the outbreak of the uprising: 'I truly believe that the rural population of all classes, among whom these cakes spread, were as ignorant as I was myself of their real object; but it was clear they were a secret sign to be on the alert, and the minds of the people were through them kept watchful and excited. As soon as the disturbances broke out at Meerut and Delhi, the cakes explained themselves, and the people at once perceived what was expected of them.' The *chapattis* became, according to this officer, 'a kind of fiery cross, to call them [members of rural society] to action.'[7] Historians picked out the reference to the fiery cross in the nineteenth century and T. Rice Holmes compared the *chapattis* to 'the fiery cross that summoned the clans-men of Roderick to battle' (Rice Holmes: 90). For officers and historians eager to find a grand conspiracy behind the uprising, the chapatti became a very convenient peg on which to hang their theory. The circulation of *chapattis* was seen as the transmitter of the message of conspiracy and rebellion simply because the *chapattis* had circulated a few months prior to the outbreak. There were some officials within the British administration who did not see any connection between the *chapattis* and the revolt. R.H.W. Dunlop, a magistrate who had observed *chapattis* going round in his district, thought that attempts to link the *chapattis* with the uprising was 'without any sufficient grounds'. He added that 'if any connection existed it was accidental and the relationship acknowledged by other designing or ignorant persons was consequent upon the distribution and did not cause or precede it.'[8] Current

"UNTRACEABLE IN THEIR ORIGIN AND UNVERIFIABLE IN THEIR IMPORT, THE RUMOURS MOVED IN A POWERFUL CURRENT TOUCHING ON ISSUES CLOSE TO INDIGENOUS SENTIMENTS."

historiography tends to dismiss any connections between the revolt and the movement of *chapattis* (Sen: 401-03; Majumdar: 207-10). Ranajit Guha described the *chapattis* as more of a red herring rather than a fiery cross (Guha: 242) but added a new angle to the phenomenon. Guha showed, by way of William Crooke's observations of rural life in northern India, that during an epidemic some ritually consecrated object was circulated to push the disease outside the boundaries of a village or a locality or a region. This operation was called *chalawa,* which means, according to Crooke, 'passing on the malady'. North India, before the revolt, had suffered a cholera epidemic and the chapatti could have been the traditional *chalawa*. A variant of this idea was already current in the aftermath of the uprising. The acting Lieutenant-Governor of the North-Western Provinces, E.A. Reade thought the connection between the *chapattis* and the revolt arose out of a misunderstanding of a ritual. In the nineteenth century in North India, families stricken by misfortune or disease tried to get rid of it by passing it on to adjacent villages in the form of food or clothing. Reade thought that it was the nervous reaction of J.R. Colvin, the Lieutenant-Governor of NWP, which raised the bogey of sedition and aggravated the atmosphere of panic and alarm (Bayly, 1996: 321-22). Clearly, the chapatti could have meant different things to different people. Guha summed up thus:

> The symbolic agent of an epidemic in the countryside it [the chapatti] took on an added meaning as the carrier of an imminent but undefined political holocaust ... As an omen it looked ahead of events, and in an atmosphere charged with growing unrest in agrarian communities and army barracks it transmitted the rebellion in anticipation by sounding a tocsin for all to hear but none to understand why. (Guha: 246)

The exact significance of the *chapattis* remains a bit of an enigma. But as one contemporary rightly commented, 'If the transmission of these cakes was only intended to create a mysterious uneasiness, that object was gained.'[9] It was remembered by an Indian contemporary as an 'event which undoubtedly created a feeling of great alarm in the native mind throughout Hindoostan.'[10]

The sense of 'great alarm' among the people of North India was heightened by wandering religious men and fakirs in towns which later became major seats of rebellion. In Lucknow, Maulavi Ahmadullah Shah arrived in Lucknow in November 1856 and gave a call for jihad against the Company's rule. People flocked to listen to him. A man called Qadir Ali Shah posed as a saint and raised a force of 12,000 men and planned an uprising against the British. Other messiahs were also reported to be spreading anti-British sentiments (Mukherjee, 1984: 36-37). Reports of religious leaders visiting other areas and even the barracks of sepoys poured in (FSUP: I:397-99; Bayly, 1996: 320).

Omens, rumours, the circulation of mysterious objects and the message spread by religious men excited sepoys and the common people in North India. In sepoy lines and in villages and towns, these matters were discussed and may have even driven men to action. But the fact that prophecies, rumours and the message of rebellion caught on was related to more material disaffections engendered by British rule in North India.

PRICE OF ENGLISHNESS

'BECAUSE WE WERE TOO ENGLISH the great crisis arose,' so wrote Kaye in the introduction to his magisterial *A History of the Sepoy War in India, 1857-58*. The observation is pregnant with suggestion and significance. It relates the revolt of 1857 to the nature and impact of British rule in India as it articulated itself in the first half of the nineteenth century. The causes were embedded in the way the British saw themselves in India and in the way they wanted to rule the country that they had conquered by the sword. Kaye knew, and most serious historians after him have concurred, that an uprising as violent and as long-lasting as the one North India witnessed between the summers of 1857 and 1858 could not be explained by a simple greased cartridge and the disaffection that it caused among the sepoys of the Bengal Army. The resistance to British rule in 1857-58 had a very strong civilian component (Chaudhuri: 1957) and this calls for an explanation more complex than the cartridges of the Enfield rifle. For analytical convenience, these sections focus on the causes of the revolt of 1857 under the following heads: pre-conditions; precipitants; and triggers.[11]

> **"IT WAS THE HISTORIAN KAYE WHO REMARKED THE REVOLT WAS THE PRICE THE BRITISH PAID FOR BEING TOO BRITISH. BRITISH POLICIES WERE DIRECTLY LINKED TO THE REBELLION."**

Pre-conditions

In the second half of the eighteenth century when the British were establishing their power in Bengal, Bombay and in Madras, they took great care not to intervene in Indian society. The drive to maximize revenue from their newly conquered provinces occupied the minds of administrators in India and in the English East India Company's headquarters in Leadenhall Street, London. The British were cautious not to interfere in social customs because that might unsettle their subjects and impede trade. Influenced by Edmund Burke, the British in the late eighteenth century saw India as an ancient civilization with its own traditions and as one that ran smoothly and needed no reform (Metcalf, 1964: 6-7). The policy of non-intervention was set aside in the first half of the nineteenth century and administrators were seized by the project of improvement and an agenda of reform. This zeal emanated from developments in Britain. The defeat of Napoleon and the emergence of England as the 'workshop of the world' had given to the British a sense of superiority which was impregnated with ideas of liberalism and evangelicalism. This produced a new aggressive attitude, which the French, who adopted it later, called that of *la mission civilisatrice*. India was to be reformed in the image of Britain. Commenting on this policy, Eric Stokes wrote: 'The missionaries of English civilization in India stood openly for a policy of "assimilation" ... The physical and mental distance separating East and West was to be annihilated by the discoveries of science, by commercial intercourse, and by transplanting the genius of English laws and English education' (Stokes, 1959: xiii-xiv).

The shift in policy had strong economic underpinnings. The Industrial Revolution in Britain brought about a fundamental change in the economic relationship of India with Britain. From a provider of tribute, which facilitated the trade of the East India Company, India came to be looked upon as a supplier of raw materials and as a vast market to be conquered and exploited for the benefit of British industries and the British economy. To ensure this new economic relationship, political power in India had to be used to create the necessary conditions of law and order and policies had to be directed towards creating a class of people in India who would buy British goods and serve as bulwarks of the new and emerging empire. This thrust was clear from a speech made by one of the principal proponents of the policy of reform, Thomas Babington Macaulay, to the House of Commons on 10 July 1833: '...far better for us that the people of India were well governed and independent of us, than ill governed and subject to us; that they were ruled by their kings, but wearing our broadcloth, and working with our cutlery, than that they were performing their salaams to English collectors and English magistrates, but were too ignorant to value, or too poor to buy, English manufactures' (Metcalf, 1964: 12). In the same speech, Macaulay said that this transformation would be the 'pacific triumphs of reason over barbarism' (Clive, 1972: 232). The statement contained the suggestion that education and enlightenment would be the motors of reform. The advocates of reform were involved in a pedagogical mission.

The era of reform was inaugurated in 1828 with the arrival of Lord William Bentinck in Calcutta as the new Governor-General of India. But even earlier there had been disapproving voices aimed at the promotion of Orientalist learning followed by the Company. In 1792, Charles Grant, later to become a member of the Court of Directors, had proposed in a tract that English rather than the vernaculars should become the medium of instruction in India and that language alone would provide a gateway to reason for the Indians and civilize them.[12] The Charter Act of 1813 stipulated that a sum of Rs 100,000 each year should be set aside for 'the revival and improvement of literature and the encouragement of the learned natives of India, and for the introduction and promotion of a knowledge of the sciences among the inhabitants of the British territories of India.'[13] Already with the reforming zeal of Bentinck nearly two decades away, the emphasis on the sciences is clear although nothing came of this stipulation in the Act. The Court of Directors discouraged the setting up of new colleges. The point about introducing the sciences was even more forcefully made by none other than James Mill who in 1819 had been appointed assistant examiner for the Court of Directors of the East India Company. In 1824 in a despatch, Mill wrote that the 'great end should not have been to teach Hindoo learning, but useful learning' (Clive: 347).

Mill's agenda found an independent echo in a letter that Ram Mohun Roy, the founder of the Atmiya Sabha and a great syncretist, had written in November 1823 to Lord Amherst, the then Governor-General. Ram Mohun wrote to protest against the proposal to set up a Sanskrit College in Calcutta. What India needed, he said was a more useful and liberal system of education based on the European model 'embracing mathematics, natural philosophy, chemistry and anatomy, with other useful sciences.'[14] Earlier, in 1817, Ram Mohun Roy had been one of the affluent and upper-caste Bengalis who had taken the initiative to establish Hindu College for the education of their children. The founders had insisted that the college should not teach Hindu theology and metaphysics but western history, literature and the natural sciences. In the words of one historian, the original aim of Hindu College was to impart 'useful knowledge from the West ... without ethnocentric bias' (Kopf: 181). The institution received some government patronage till it was taken over by the government in 1855 and renamed Presidency College. There was thus in Calcutta in the early nineteenth century a body of Indian opinion, articulated by influential and wealthy people, who were otherwise conservative, favouring the introduction of western education in English. This served to facilitate the transformation that men like Bentinck and Macaulay wanted to bring about. The introduction of English spread even to Oriental colleges like the Calcutta Madrassa and the Sanskrit College at Calcutta and Benares and the Agra College (Mitra: 432). The famous Educational Despatch of 1854 drawn up by Charles Wood, President, Board of Control, insisted that western learning was superior to Oriental and was to form the basis of education in India. The emphasis was on the dissemination of 'useful and practical knowledge' (Metcalf, 1964: 24).

If among the wealthy Bengalis there was some sort of consensus about the kind of education their sons should receive in Hindu College, changes in social customs and rituals proved to be divisive. The two major legislations introduced by the government before the revolt, were of native provenance but support to it was by no means unanimous. In 1829, largely at the initiative of Ram Mohun Roy, the government introduced a legislation abolishing *sati*, the custom by which a Hindu widow immolated herself on the pyre of her dead husband. Even though Bentinck announced 'I write and feel as a legislator for the Hindus and as I believe many enlightened Hindus think and feel,' the law aroused a great deal of hostility even among some enlightened Bengalis (Metcalf: 26-27). Conservative Bengalis could accept their sons learning English and the western sciences but they did not approve of a direct intervention into their religious and social customs. Ram Mohun's recommendation for the abolition of *sati* was based on a particular reading of the Hindu scriptures and this allowed scope for not only disagreement but even for a vituperative debate. The process was replicated when Iswarchandra Vidyasagar, an orthodox Brahmin pundit, basing himself on a very close reading of the Hindu sacred texts recommended that Hindu widows should be allowed to remarry. In 1855, the government passed the Hindu Widow Remarriage Act.[15] These reforms were taken as evidence that the British wanted to intervene in Indian society not only to change it but also to Christianize it.

This latter gloss emerged because the thrust towards western education came to be associated with the work of Christian missionaries. English schools mushroomed under the fostering care of the Calcutta Diocesan Committee, the Church Missionary Society, London Missionary Society, the Church of Scotland and so on. Alexander Duff, a missionary, summed the purpose of these schools as, 'to kill Hinduism by striking at its brain, Calcutta' (Mitra: 432). The evangelical zeal of the missionaries was a source of great anxiety for the Indians. Hand in hand with western learning and English came the Bible. It was introduced not only in the schools run by the missionaries but also in government schools. Henry Carre Tucker, a missionary in north India, noted approvingly that in the free school in Kanpur and in the school established by Jayanarain Ghoshal in Benares instruction was carried out on 'a strict Christian basis'. One army officer wrote to Lord Ellenborough, the Governor-General between 1842 and 1844 that the evangelists wanted 'to Christianize India all at once' and added that 'the natives have now good reason for supposing this to be done.' Sir Syed Ahmed Khan, not known for his hostility to British rule, pointed to the dangers involved in the way the Bible was taught. He said that in some of the missionary schools students were asked, 'Who is your God? Who is your redeemer?' and the answers were supposed to be in accordance with the Christian catechism (Sen:10).

Ordinary Indians did not make a distinction between the aims of the missionaries and the intentions of the government. Both were alien and some of the practices and laws introduced by the government seemed to confirm suspicions that the government was not averse to the idea of conversion. A Bengali clergyman who worked in Fatehpur wrote, 'The prisoners in the jail were also daily instructed in Christianity and general knowledge by a Christian teacher, and every Sabbath morning the Gospel was preached by me. This privilege was granted by our pious magistrate. The judge and the magistrate, as well as other gentlemen, took a deep interest in the mission, and helped us with their prayers, good advice and pecuniary aid. When the number of native converts began to increase, six of them at the suggestion of the late Honourable Mr Colvin, became small farmers' (Sen:10). Thus not only was the local administration fully involved in proselytizing the prisoners, the Lieutenant-Governor of the North-western Provinces had rewarded some of those who had converted. This only confirmed the impression that the government wanted to convert its subjects to Christianity. The suspicion was strengthened when by a regulation passed in 1845 common messing was made compulsory in jails. For high caste prisoners, this meant a direct transgression of caste rules. They were forced to eat with men with whom inter-dining was not permitted. As a result, when a Hindu was released from prison, he was considered by his family to have lost caste and tabooed by them. The discontent growing from this – there was a riot in Benares – was aggravated by reports that common dining would be extended to the army. Muslims too were disaffected by prison regulations because as soon as a Muslim entered a prison his beard and moustache were shaved off (Sen: 11). The fears about the government's intentions with regards to interfering in native customs with an agenda for conversion to Christianity were heightened by the Act XXI of 1850 by which converts were allowed to inherit ancestral property. Under both Hindu and Islamic law an apostate forfeited his right to inherit property. The Act made no mention of Christianity but only embodied the principle that change of religion should not entail civil disability. But for all practical purposes it benefited Christian converts. The Hindus criticized the Act because they said a convert was not permitted to perform the last rites required of the inheritor and for the spiritual well being of the deceased (Metcalf, 1964: 27-28).

To the Indian mind the introduction of western learning, the attempt to interfere in religious customs, the activities of the missionaries and the official support the latter received, all pointed to the evil intentions of the rulers. In the various proclamations of the rebel leaders, which we shall analyze later, these elements came for criticism and attack. They prepared the ground for disaffection.

Disaffection also had more material dimensions and these were related to the methods of land settlement and revenue collection that the British introduced in India. The revolt of 1857 was concentrated in the area loosely referred to as the Gangetic plain. In British administrative terms it consisted of the North-Western Provinces and the kingdom of Awadh. This was the core area of the rebellion. This part of North India was acquired by the British through annexation and treaties in a number of stages. In 1801, the Nawab of Awadh handed over to Lord Wellesley a large chunk of his territories. This consisted of the districts of Bareilly, Moradabad, Farrukhabad, Etawah, Kanpur, Allahabad and Gorakhpur. These ceded districts encircled the Nawab's domain on three sides. Thus by 1801, British rule had entered the heart of the Gangetic plain. In 1803, the remaining districts of the Ganges-Jamuna-Doab, together with Agra and Delhi, were annexed by Lord Lake after he defeated the Maratha chieftain, Daulat Rao Sindhia. Together these came to be known as the Ceded and Conquered Provinces and later from 1836 as the North-Western Provinces. In 1856, Awadh was annexed.

The first task that faced the British when an area was brought under their rule was the collection of land revenue. This was absolutely vital since only greater revenues and greater trade could justify the expansion of dominions. But the collection of land revenue and the establishment of a land revenue administration and policy in the Gangetic plain did not prove to be easy as this new site of British power was littered with the debris of the practices and conventions of the previous regime. These were invariably a source of confusion. In India, it has been noted:

> ... for centuries, landed property had been the very foundation of both wealth and prestige, where all aspects of culture, including religion, had land as their common denominator and the relation between producers, proprietors and the state had evolved over time into a bewildering variety of local patterns according to differences in the regional structures of dominance and economies.[16]

British land revenue policy in the NWP and in central India was to choose a group from within the rural society on whom it could entrust the responsibility of collecting and paying the land revenue. On this choice, would depend the nature of land rights and the wielding of power in the rural world. In Bengal, the British had solved the problem by giving the responsibility to the zamindars. In the NWP, it was not that easy and the situation was aggravated by variations in regional practices and patterns of land-holding of which the British were initially utterly ignorant. Ignorance resulted in a period of trial and error before a coherent land revenue policy was decided upon. The lack of knowledge about the rural world made the dependence on local informants inevitable. Such informants – the revenue officials and record-keepers of the previous political dispensation – were often reluctant to part with the knowledge that they considered to be their expertise.

For any land revenue policy to become viable in India, it was necessary for the British to have information regarding the extent of agricultural production, the value of such production, the regulations and procedures of extracting the peasant's surplus by the state or by intermediaries on the state's behalf, the nature of land tenures and property structure, the methods of account-keeping and the laws that governed the complex relationship between the state, the peasant and the land. In the pre-British administration, the *tahsildar*, the *patwari* and the *qunungo* were the repository of such information. The British when they began taking their first steps in administering their newly conquered territories in North India could not take for granted the co-operation of these officials. Settlement officers noted the difficulties they faced in acquiring information. British administration, newly arrived, had not succeeded in displacing the older bureaucracy and replacing it by its own officials. Members of the older political order, naturally suspicious of the British, refused to give up the knowledge, which was their special preserve (Mukherjee, 1998: 12-14).

These obstacles together with the ignorance of the new rulers made the first forays into land revenue administration very haphazard. But the early revenue experiments in North India had one common element – over-assessment was built into the revenue settlements. This was inextricably linked to the way the British viewed their territorial acquisitions. Kaye wrote:

> Officers trained in the essential business of "settlement operations" had learnt that their efficiency as public servants was estimated in accordance with their success attending their efforts to screw up the revenue of their several districts to the highest possible pitch of productiveness. As long as the money was got, there was very little thought of the effect that might be produced on the minds of the people by the manner of getting it. The black-and-white of demonstrable figures was greater in their minds than the animosities and resentments of an over-taxed people.
>
> (Kaye: iii: 425-26)

Over-assessment was particularly marked in the first revenue experiments in the Ceded and Conquered Provinces. For the area as a whole (exclusive of Delhi), the land revenue demand rose from Rs 1,88,12,617 in 1803-04 to Rs 2,97,30, 997 in 1817-18, a rise of 50 per cent in 14 years (Metcalf: 1979: 55). Arrears of payment also mounted and the government had to take recourse to the forced sale of lands to recover the arrears. Contemporary observers and later historians described the upheaval in the property rights as 'a very extensive and melancholy revolution.' But many of the sales were fraudulent and benefited the government officials and bankers who negotiated the transactions. Fraud was most rampant in the districts of Gorakhpur, Allahabad and Kanpur. Elsewhere, in the Doab and in Rohilkhand, property advertised for sale remained with the original owners. The land market was imperfect and few buyers showed up at the auctions; consequently, the government was obliged to buy up the estates at a nominal price (Metcalf: 1979: 56-57). Thus when the revised settlements began under Bird and Thomason, land was by and large held by those groups who had held it before annexation. The real upheaval began after the revised settlements which fixed the rights of all those on the land and thus endowed on land a value it had never had before.

The process of revision was initiated in 1819 by a Minute prepared by Holt Mackenzie, the Secretary to Government in the Territorial Department. The premise of the Minute, which was to serve as the basis for revenue administration in North India, was the ignorance of the British officials about rural conditions. Mackenzie recommended a detailed survey of the rights, interests and privileges of all classes connected with the soil. But even before the survey was begun, Mackenzie asserted that the village coparcenary bodies were sole owners of the land and therefore entitled to a full proprietary title. The survey was thus started with a bias against *taluqdars* and other intermediaries whose claims, Mackenzie insisted, should be ignored. Mackenzie's recommendations were incorporated into Regulation VII of 1822. Given the resources and the manpower of the government, it was impossible to carry out the detailed inquiry that Mackenzie and Regulation VII had recommended. Estimates tended to be haphazard and the settlement of 1822 ended up hiking up land revenue to the

> **"ORDINARY INDIANS DID NOT MAKE A DISTINCTION BETWEEN THE AIMS OF THE MISSIONARIES AND THE INTENTIONS OF THE BRITISH GOVERNMENT. BOTH WERE ALIEN."**

highest possible amount. The effects of over-assessment were compounded by an agrarian depression, which hit North India after 1828 (Siddiqi: ch. 5). Between 1828-33, because of the fall in prices, the real value of the assessment increased by about 22 per cent (Siddiqi: 173).

The agrarian conditions dictated that the process of revision be speeded up even if all of Mackenzie's conditions about securing detailed knowledge were not fulfilled. The driving force in hastening the revision was the Governor-General, Lord William Bentinck himself. The task of carrying out the revision was entrusted to R.M. Bird. Bird shared Mackenzie's bias against the *taluqdars* and all other kinds of privilege connected with land. Among the hardest hit were the holders of various types of revenue-free grants. Bird believed these were a luxury the British could not afford. He further believed that the holders of these grants had no rights over the land and were mere revenue intermediaries. Thus the resumption of these holdings meant the ouster of the previous holders. By 1840, the government had resumed about 1,750,000 acres with a revenue demand of Rs 23 lakhs (Metcalf: 1979: 68-69).

Equally adversely affected by the revision were the *taluqdars* towards whom Bird and his team had an attitude of hostility. They completely ignored the fact that many of the *taluqdars* had held their estates for many generations and were closely connected with the land and the village community. The *taluqdars* were broken up and dispossessed after 1835. By the 1850s the *taluqdars* had lost most of the sources of income. But this is not to say that they had lost their status in rural society or the influence they had over their tenants. They retained their position of dominance in the rural areas as was to be demonstrated in the events of 1857. The revenue settlements thus created a body of disgruntled but influential people who remained a force of consequence in rural society.

The revised settlement under Bird and then Thomason gave to the village communities proprietary titles and lifted the presence of the *taluqdar* from them. But this did not mean that a new age of prosperity had dawned for the peasants. One study of agrarian relations in the NWP has summarized the situation thus:

> Indeed throughout the 1830s, and into the years of the midcentury, the combination of commercial depression and continued harsh assessments drove them increasingly into debt, and into arrears on their revenue payments. At the same time the settlement brought with it a new and more precise definition of all landed rights. The result was a dramatic and altogether unforeseen rise in the enforced transfer of property through the agency of the civil courts. (Metcalf: 1979:105)

Apart from the sale of lands for arrears of revenue, land was also sold under pressure to raise money to pay the revenue or to meet the demand of creditors. There was another process through which land changed hands. The land settlement defined land rights in a very precise way. Consequently, there were enforced sales of lands through the agency of the civil courts.

Sales for arrears in revenue were concentrated in the Doab districts – Aligarh to Allahabad – and to the adjacent districts of Bundelkhand, Hamirpur and Banda. Most of these districts were involved in commercial agriculture in the 1820s and 1830s and were thus highly assessed. They were also severely hit by the agricultural depression of 1829-1830. The revised settlement gave the landholder an exclusive and transferable title, which was equivalent to rights of ownership. Land thus became a valuable asset, which could be mortgaged and could also be transferred by a court decree on the occasion of default. The landholders thus became more creditworthy. The prominence of the moneylender in the rural world of the nineteenth century was predicated on this. Sales by court decree began in the 1830s and rose rapidly in the next decade when they were averaging about 2000 cases per annum. In the depressed districts of the Doab, however, creditors were not too eager to take possession of debtors' properties. They preferred to leave the title with the owner and let the interest payments mount. Only after the depression had lifted and the value of the land had risen in the mid 1840s did the creditors force the issue and bring land to sale so 'that they might buy in themselves and obtain a valuable investment for their money.' The return of commerce and the revival of commercial agriculture made the heavy assessments easier to bear but the transformation of land into a valuable asset made the landholder more susceptible to borrowing and thus increased the dominance of the moneylender in the rural world (Metcalf: 1979: ch.v).

Some features of the consequences of these land sales need to be emphasized. One is that the sales saw the rise of new landholding groups. A large portion of land went to families whose principal occupation was recorded as moneylending

“IN AWADH BRITISH LAND-REVENUE POLICY INITIATED A NEAR REVOLUTION IN LAND RIGHTS AND THE NATURE AND THE LEVEL OF THE ASSESSMENT. THIS LAND-REVENUE POLICY HIT THE TALUQDARS VERY HARD.”

or other non-agricultural occupations. Rajputs, the principal controllers of land in the pre-British period, were the biggest losers. Historians, as Metcalf is quick to point out, (Metcalf: 1979:135) may have exaggerated the extent of the upheaval caused by heavy assessments and distress sales but there is no reason to underestimate the economic and emotional impact of the loss of land on those who were affected. In 1854, the Board of Revenue commented, 'In no country in the world probably do landed tenures so certainly, constantly and extensively change hands. These mutations are effecting a rapid and complete revolution in the position of the ancient proprietors of the soil.' The calculation was that 10 per cent of agricultural land had passed to moneylenders. Yet official policy refused to intervene in the free trade in land. Apart from an ideological commitment to *laissez faire*, there was the fear the legislative interference might upset rural credit and jeopardize the payment of land revenue (Stokes:1984: 52). The moneylender was emerging as a major prop of the British administration. For those who lost their land, it meant both fall in income and loss of *izzat*. The affected could also identify the new *sarkar* (government/ruler) as the perpetrator of the loss. Agrarian policy and the consequent change became a source of discontent.

In the area immediately south of the Jamuna and running towards the Narmada, the British as they annexed the territory followed the policy of resuming all revenue-free grants wherever possible. In the districts of Jalaun, Hamirpur and Banda, alienable proprietary title was introduced. The impact of this was disastrous on tenures. Titles were transferred rapidly and the gainers were the *mushtari* (auction purchasers). Assessment in Bundelkhand had been high ever since the settlement of 1817 and even in 1840, the collector of Banda, R.N. Cust, was lamenting the 'utterly ruined and shaken' condition of the village communities. Like in the NWP, British policy was a threat to intermediaries. The *thakurs* managed to win recognition, after a fight, as a zamindar. In Jhansi, annexed in 1854, the British avoided the perils of over-assessment. But in the Saugor and Narmada Territories, acquired in 1818 and administered as part of the NWP, over-assessment was marked, especially in the narrow valley of the Narmada River. In Hoshangabad, for example, in the 1820s, the demand was as high as threefold the Maratha figure and had to be moderated in the next decade. Population was less and land abundant. Thus when the Saugor Proclamation of 1854 accorded saleable proprietary title to the *malguzar* (revenue payers), this was meaningless as no landlord tenures or landlord rent had emerged (Stokes:1984: 68-78). Thus this area was also adversely affected by British land revenue policy.

North of the Ganges, in what was the kingdom of Awadh till 1856, British land revenue policy initiated a near revolution in land rights and the nature and level of assessment. This was a region where *taluqdars* were very strongly entrenched and had been so for many generations. The relationship between taluqdar and peasant was strong and fortified by ties of dependence and reciprocity (Mukherjee: 1984: 24-26). The importance of the *taluqdar* in the rural world of Awadh needs to be underlined. Before the annexation, *taluqdars* held about 67 per cent of the villages in Awadh. In southern Awadh where the dominant Rajput lineages had been strong for two centuries, the *taluqdars* held more than 70 per cent of the villages and in the far-flung north where the Nawab's authority had never effectively penetrated, *taluqdari* holdings were as high as 80 to 90 per cent (Mukherjee: 1984: 26-27). The emblem of the *taluqdar's* power was the fort, and these dotted the countryside (Mukherjee: 1984:175-83). British administrators carried over from NWP into Awadh their prejudices against taluqdars. The latter were apprehensive of British intentions. Sleeman, who had toured Awadh extensively, wrote in 1853:

> In 1801 when the Oude territory was divided, and half taken by us and half left to Oude, the landed aristocracy of each were about equal. Now hardly a family of this class remains in our half, while in Oude it remains unimpaired. Everybody in Oude believes those families to have been systematically crushed.[17]

Apprehension became reality when the administration immediately after the take-over ordered a wholesale destruction and disarming of the forts.

The bias against the *taluqdars* was evident in the way the land was settled. It was assumed that Awadh and the NWP shared the same features and thus the special character of the Awadh *taluqdar* was ignored. Land revenue officers were directed to follow the principles laid down by Bird and Thomason and to settle the land with the actual proprietors of the soil and to do away with the *taluqdars*, who were seen as an imposition between the actual proprietor and the government. Thus armed by policy prescriptions, British revenue officers stirred up, in the words of one officer, 'every ancient claim or title of a right that we could discover in every village of Oudh. No matter how remote the title it was allowed.' Through this process, across Awadh, the holdings of *taluqdars* were nearly halved by the Summary Settlement of 1856-57. Prior to annexation, the *taluqdars* had held 67 per cent of the villages; after the settlement of 1856-57, their holdings were reduced to 38 per cent. In the districts of southern Awadh where the *taluqdars* had held close to 70 per cent of the villages, they suffered enormously. Their holdings fell in most cases to 30 per cent and in one district to 17 per cent from 74 per cent. Up in the northern reaches, where the *taluqdars* had held over 80 per cent of the villages, their holdings also fell dramatically (Mukherjee:1984: 53-59 and Table 7).

It could be argued that the losses suffered by the *taluqdars* and the consequent disaffection were offset by the gains of the actual proprietors with whom the land was settled and their consequent loyalty to British rule. This did not happen. This was because of the presence of over-assessment at the local level. At an aggregate level, the province was assessed at a level lower than it had been before 1856. But even this assessment was not considered moderate and had to be reduced after the uprising. In comparing the pre-British and British revenue assessments, it needs to be remembered that the British revenue demands were following upon many years of rack-renting by the Nawabi administration. Thus, while the British revenue demands could appear moderate in *relative* terms, i.e., compared to previous assessments, they could have been pitched too high in *absolute* terms, i.e., when compared to what remained of the revenue-paying capacities of the area. Senior British officers were aware of this and often asked their subordinates to bear this in mind when making the assessment (Mukherjee: 1984: 51).

It is also important to emphasize that the evidence of local level over-assessment comes from those areas where features of reciprocity and complementarity between *taluqdar* and peasant was most marked. This meant that the peasants lost their lord and protector and were faced with the impersonal land revenue administration and laws of the British, something alien. The moral economy of the rural world of Awadh was disrupted. The *taluqdar* lost his land, his fort, his power and his prestige. The peasant was faced with a system with which he was unfamiliar and perceived as alien. The removal of the *taluqdars* had a widespread impact. The *taluqdars* had never used their wealth for any productive purpose but the wealth had supported a lifestyle in which patronage, protection and loyalty were important. The *taluqdars'* removal meant the end of that ambience; it also meant that the agrarian surplus, which had maintained that world, was now extracted by the bureaucratic machinery of the British Raj. From the network of patronage and cooperation the rural world was exposed to the system of colonial revenue policy and its bureaucratic implementation. The shift frightened peasants who told Sleeman that they did not understand British laws and rules and preferred the custom of the villages to the British courts. They were emphatic in their support to 'native' rule over British administration.[18]

Thus, across North India, in the areas which were to emerge as the principal theatres of the rebellion, British social and economic policy had created the grounds of popular disaffection. Large sections of the Indian population had reasons to be suspicious of British intentions. British policies were instrumental in the dissolution of an old and familiar world. It would be unsympathetic to expect that those adversely affected by the policies would sit down to calculate if the new dispensation would be better than the world they had lost. The alienness of the new regime was best captured in a folk song of the time: 'The British began to measure the land in iron chains.'[19]

Precipitants

This sense of loss accumulating over two or three decades was compounded by aspects of British policy under the Governor-General Lord Dalhousie (1848-1856). Under Dalhousie, British annexation in India entered a new phase. He abandoned the idea of expansion through conquest. The Union Jack was no longer carried forward by victorious armies but by the diktats of a supreme power which saw itself in a position to set its own terms and conditions even if these ran counter to Indian traditions and customs. Dalhousie decided that Indian princes, all of whom were enjoying British protection and thus nominally under British tutelage, would lose the right to rule if they did not have male heirs to succeed them. He chose not to recognize adopted sons. The absence of a biological male heir, Dalhousie decreed, would mean that the right to rule had lapsed and that the British as the paramount power had the right to annex the territory into their dominion.[20] Thus under this dispensation a number of old princely houses and their territories went under the hammer. Satara and Nagpur, traditional Maratha strongholds and focus of popular loyalties, were the first to go. Jhansi followed and the Peshwa's adopted son, Nana Sahib, was set aside.

The cases of Jhansi and Nana Sahib deserve special mention, as the latter and the Rani of Jhansi, Lakshmibai, became important leaders of the revolt. Jhansi was a small state in Bundelkhand in Central India, which had been given the status of a kingdom by the East India Company. By a treaty in 1817 the British had guaranteed the kingdom to Ramchandra Rao, his heirs and his successors. In the early 1840s, Gangadhar Rao, became the king, and he died heirless in 1853. But the day before his death, he had adopted a son and had asked the British political agent of Jhansi to look after his son and widow and to allow the latter to run the kingdom as a regent. Dalhousie rejected this plea on the ground that Jhansi had never been an independent sovereign state and had been raised to the status of a kingdom by the Company. He incorporated Jhansi into the British territories in March 1854 and promised the Rani a pension. Lakshmibai initially refused to accept the pension, and when she reconciled herself to accepting it she found it encumbered by a number of deductions on account of her husband's debts. She argued that these were the liabilities of the state, a position that the British administration refused to accept. Her husband had left behind Rs 6 lakhs in the treasury, and the British government held this in trust till her son attained majority. But the government refused to give the Rani Rs 1 lakh from this trust to perform the son's sacred thread ceremony. It further hurt the sentiments of the Rani and her subjects by introducing cow slaughter, which had previously not been allowed in Jhansi (Sen: 264-67).

The setting aside of Nana Sahib was somewhat unique since it involved no acquisition of territory even though it was an extension of the Doctrine of Lapse. After Peshwa Baji Rao II, the head of the Maratha power, had surrendered to the British in June 1818, he had been asked to retire to Bithur, near Kanpur, with a pension of Rs 8 lakh. Baji Rao was also given a *jagir* (land grant) tenable during his lifetime. Baji Rao was childless but had adopted two sons, of whom Nana Sahib was the eldest. It had been made clear to the Peshwa that the pension was 'purely personal to himself': adopted sons and other claimants would only have claims to Baji Rao's private property. By his will Baji Rao made Nana Sahib his sole successor. After Baji Rao's death in 1851, the pension stopped much to the financial embarrassment of Nana Sahib. The latter petitioned the government for a continuation of his father's pension. But Lord Dalhousie believed that the Peshwa had been paid enough during his lifetime, and those that remained had no claims whatsoever on the consideration of the British government. More petitions and pleading, including a memorial to the Court of Directors in London, did not alter the decision taken by the Governor-General. The British government compounded the sense of injury felt by Nana Sahib by bringing the inhabitants of Bithur (i.e. the Peshwa's family and retainers) under the jurisdiction of the civil and criminal courts at Kanpur. The pecuniary embarrassment thus merged with a fall in status. The old order had finally departed from Bithur and from the life of the Nana Sahib (Gupta: 1-30).

The most dramatic of Lord Dalhousie's annexations was the takeover of Awadh. Here the Doctrine of Lapse could not be invoked so Dalhousie invoked misrule to renege on a treaty the British government had made with the kings of Awadh in 1837. In a sense, by annexing Awadh, Dalhousie brought to a logical conclusion the subordination of the kingdom to British political and economic control that had been initiated after the battle of Baksar in 1764. The plank of annexation – misrule – was based on reports of British administrators like W.H. Sleeman and James Outram that provided graphic accounts of the prevailing law and order. Commenting on Outram's report, Dalhousie wrote:

> It seems impossible that the home authorities can any longer hesitate to overthrow this fortress of corruption and infamous misgovernment. I should not mind doing it as a parting *coup*.[21]

Earlier in 1851, he had described Awadh as 'a cherry which will drop into our mouths some day. It has long been ripening.'[22] It is true that conditions in Awadh could not meet the standards of good administration set by Britons in the nineteenth century. The latter saw the 'misrule' as a function of the king's inability to rule. This was definitely

Dalhousie's own understanding of the situation and this can be taken as being typical of the time.[23] What Dalhousie and most of his contemporaries and peers overlooked was the fact that the king's inability to rule was related to the nature of the British alliance with Awadh. The treaty that Lord Wellesley had imposed on the rulers of Awadh in 1801 had had an adverse impact on the Awadh administration. It had made the administration dependent on British troops for the enforcement of law and order. After 1830, when non-interference in the affairs of the native rulers had become the official policy, British troops had been withdrawn. The kings of Awadh were thus left without any support and bereft of any machinery for the maintenance of law and order. The kingdom sank into misrule and this became the pretext of annexation. The inability of the kings to rule was a direct outcome of British policy. As a recent writer has noted:

> With the subsidiary alliance drawn tightly about him, he could not ignore the British and act as before. But he had neither the training nor the military force to act upon the injunction of his European advisers. So the Nawabs who succeeded Saadat Ali Khan, one after the other, increasingly abandoned the attempt to govern and retired into the *zanana* where they amused themselves with wine, women and poetry. The sensuous life … did not reflect sheer perversity or weakness of character on the part of the Nawabs. Indolence was rather the only appropriate response to the situation in which the princes of Oudh were placed. (Metcalf, 1979: 39- 40)

This statement spells out the political background of misgovernment in Awadh. However, there was more to misgovernment than British political presence in and around Awadh. Since 1765 the British relations with Awadh had an economic dimension, which drained the kingdom of resources and served as a source of economic dislocation. Trade controlled by the Company or by European traders had channelled economic resources away from Awadh. This had also contributed to misgovernment (Mukherjee, 1982). A specialist on the history of Awadh has noted that after 1801 Awadh was important to the British not for what it could do, but for what it had to offer (Reeves, 1971: 6). It is thus not surprising that governors-general saw Awadh as something to eat. Wellesley promised London a 'supper of Oudh' (Phillips, 1961: 104) and Dalhousie saw it as a ripe cherry.

The impact of these annexations was devastating. The princes feared for their territory and their status. They were no longer certain that their loyalty to the British would be a guarantee against annexation. They were no longer sure of being treated honourably by the Company. Their disgruntlement was articulated variously. The king of Awadh, Wajid Ali Shah, refused to sign the treaty that was offered to him because he felt it was demeaning. He had to be removed to Calcutta. When he left Lucknow for Calcutta via Kanpur, many of his subjects singing dirges followed him up to Kanpur (Mukherjee, 1984: 36). The Rani of Jhansi, it was said, had announced, '*meri Jhansi nahi dungi*' (I will not surrender my Jhansi). The removal of kings hurt the sentiments of the people.

A series of policy measures initiated by the British administration affecting society, economy and the polity alienated the people of North India. The British introduced the policies to reform society, to streamline the land revenue administration and to rid the country of rulers who did not meet British Victorian standards of governance. For the British, the reforms may have been necessary to carry out what they considered to be their civilizing mission in India but to most Indians, save for a miniscule group of western educated Bengalis in Calcutta, they appeared as unfair and unjust interventions into tradition and custom aimed at undermining what Indians considered sacred. They found the measures too alien. A group of peasants told Sleeman, 'we cannot understand the *ain* and *kanoon* (rules and regulations)' (Sleeman, ii: 66-67). A familiar way of life was disappearing and this affected people more than the assumed and ascribed benefits of British rule.

Another set of precipitants for the rebellion came from where it began, the army. The process of recruiting Indians into the army of the English East India Company began in the middle of the eighteenth century, when the Company decided to become a player in the politics of South India and Bengal. The Bengal Army can be dated to the period after the battle of Plassey (1757) when the Company began recruiting soldiers in Bengal and Bihar to create a proper standing army. Before that, around 1756, Robert Clive, after his arrival in Calcutta from Madras, had raised the first battalion of about 500 sepoys, trained and dressed like British soldiers and placed under a British officer. The colour of their uniform gave the name Lal Paltan to the battalion. Later it came to be called Gillis ki Paltan – a name derived from that of its long-standing commander, Primrose Galliez (David: ch 3). After Plassey when the British were firmly in political control

“ACROSS NORTH INDIA, IN AREAS THAT BECAME THE PRINCIPAL THEATRES OF REBELLION, BRITISH SOCIAL AND ECONOMIC POLICY HAD CREATED THE GROUNDS FOR POPULAR DISAFFECTION.”

in Bengal, the recruiting area of the Bengal Army expanded into the rural areas of Awadh and the districts of Rae Barelli, Partapgarh, Salon, Sultanpur, Faizabad, Unnao, and so on became the principal recruiting ground for sepoys. Recruits from these areas were mostly high caste, especially Brahmin villagers (Mukherjee, 1984: 23). This high caste orientation of the sepoy army had certain important consequences for military life and discipline. The sepoys were subject to the most rigorous military discipline but the Company took care to respect and preserve the caste of the sepoys. For example, during the first Anglo-Maratha War when reinforcements had to be sent from Bengal to western India in 1779, Warren Hastings, conscious of the high caste restrictions on sea voyages, sent the sepoys by the slower overland route. Seema Alavi has suggested in her study of the sepoy army, that 'The high-caste overtones of the army … suited the political interests of the Company for it provided the requisite legitimacy to Company rule' (Alavi: 45). It made the high castes of North India appear to be active collaborators of the Company. The military administration of the Company took special measures to preserve the caste of the sepoys. The most important of these was the one concerning the sepoy's diet. Departing from the military tradition of having a common mess and a communal kitchen, the Company allowed the sepoys to carry their own cooking utensils, to cook their own food and to eat the food by themselves. Through such steps and by allowing Hindu festivals to become part of regimental life, the Company guaranteed that the sepoys' caste status was not transgressed. The Bengal Army thus became a kind of upper caste sanctuary.

But military expediency did not always allow the protection of the sepoys' caste. This was manifest in the 1820s when the Company embarked on a war against Burma. Driven by the fear that the Company would send them off to fight in Burma, sepoys of certain regiments in Barrackpore mutinied in 1824. The Company was forced to use extensive violence to quell the mutinies.[24] The sepoys' fears about losing their caste and religion as a direct consequence of the Company's policies were aggravated in the 1830s when the British rulers undertook the regime to change Indian society. The interference into social customs by the government, the introduction of western learning and English education, the annexations of Dalhousie on the basis of the Doctrine of Lapse and other planks of the era of reform appeared to the sepoys and to their families in the villages as attempts to subvert a traditional and a cherished way of life. As persons who were in the employ of the Company, the sepoys felt that they would be the first to feel the impact of the reforms and may be even coerced into accepting them. Such fears were aggravated by the changing attitudes and behaviours of their white superior officers.

Over the years, a significant change had taken place in the attitude of the white officers. Sitaram noted that:

> In those days the sahibs could speak our language much better than they do now, and they mixed more with us. Although officers today have to pass the language examination, and have to read books, they do not understand our language … The only language they learn is that of the lower orders, which they pick up from their servants, and which is unsuited to be used in polite conversation. The sahibs often used to give nautches for the regiment, and they attended all men's games. They also took us with them when they went out hunting. Nowadays they seldom attend nautches because their padre sahibs have told them it is wrong. These padre sahibs have done, and are still doing, many things to estrange the British officers from the sepoys. When I was a sepoy the captain of my company would have some of the men at his house all day long and he talked with them … [most] of us went because we liked the sahib who always treated us as if we were his children … I know that many officers nowadays only speak to their men when obliged to do so, and they show that the business is irksome and try to get rid of the sepoys as quickly as possible. (Sitaram: 24-25)

“THE HIGH CASTE ORIENTATION OF THE SEPOY ARMY HAD CERTAIN IMPORTANT CONSEQUENCES FOR MILITARY LIFE AND DISCIPLINE. MILITARY EXPEDIENCY DID NOT ALWAYS ALLOW THE PROTECTION OF THE SEPOYS' CASTE.”

Sitaram's observations not only point to the vanishing ambience of paternalism that had existed between sepoys and their white superiors but also to the suspicions that even a loyal sepoy like Sitaram harboured about the activities of the padre sahib. The sepoys and his brethren in the villages saw the Christian missionaries as instruments of estrangement, estrangement from a way of life, familiar and loved.

From a father figure, the white officer had become an impersonal disciplinarian whose behaviour was marked by a sense of superiority and of racism. One British resident in India wrote,

> The sepoy is [regarded as] an inferior creature. He is sworn at. He is treated roughly. He is spoken of as nigger. He is addressed as *suar* or pig, an epithet most opprobrious to a respectable native,

> especially the Mussulman, and which cuts him to the quick. The younger men seem to regard it as an excellent joke, as an evidence of spirit and a praiseworthy sense of superiority over the sepoy to treat him as an inferior animal.[25]

This change meant that white officers were no longer in touch with their men. They had no inkling of what the sepoys felt, what they feared and of what went on in their lines. This breakdown in communication was crucial in the making of the event that triggered off the mutinies.

The Trigger

In 1857, there were probably four types of firearms in use by the Indian soldiers of the infantry or cavalry regiments of the Bengal Army. First, there was a smooth-bore musket without any rifling. This was the Brown Bess which had been widely used in the Napoleonic wars and was the weapon in common use in the infantry regiments of the Bengal Army. But the faithful Brown Bess had undergone some modification: the percussion cap had replaced the flint as the igniter. Second, there was the Brunswick Rifle used by some of the native infantry regiments. This had two grooves of rifling. The third, an adaptation of the Brunswick rifle, was the Minie rifle, which was restricted in use. The distinctive feature of the Minie rifle was the structure of the bullet. Lastly, the cavalry used a shortened musket, which was known as a carbine.

The Minie rifle was named after a French officer who developed an elongated bullet with a metal thimble at the base that expanded when ignited. This solved certain problems regarding loading and firing that had previously existed but the metal thimble had a tendency to drive through the bullet. Experiments for further improvement were carried out at Enfield which in 1853 evolved an improved form of bullet for use with a rifled weapon, which came to be known as the Enfield Rifle or more correctly as the Enfield-Pritchett rifle (Pritchett was the man who invented the bullet). The ammunition for this was balled and was heavily greased at the base to facilitate loading. The standard practice for loading rifles was to bite the top off the cartridge and then pour the powder down the barrel. The rest of the cartridge, including the ball, was then put down the barrel with a ramrod. The grease on the Enfield cartridge became a matter of concern in India.[26]

One consideration was whether the grease would withstand the Indian climate. To test this, a consignment was sent out for sepoys to carry in their pouches. But the Commander-in-Chief of India (1850-56), General William Gomm, had warned about the grease and its implications for caste and religion in India. He had suggested that 'unless it be known that the grease employed in these cartridges is not of a nature to offend or interfere with the prejudices of caste, it will be expedient not to issue them for test to Native corps'. This warning was ignored, and after reports confirmed that the grease was not damaged by the weather in India, a shipment of greased cartridges and bullet moulds was sent out to India in 1856. After this, cartridges began to be manufactured in the arsenals at Fort William, Meerut and Dum Dum. The components of the grease were the same as what had been used in the Royal Woolwich Arsenal – five parts tallow, five parts purified fatty acids and one part wax. The type of tallow being used was never specified.[27]

In early January 1857, regiments of the Bengal Native Infantry were asked to send detachments to one of the three musketry depots in Dum Dum, Ambala or Sialkot. These detachments were to be trained and instructed to handle the new firearm and the new cartridge. It is important to underline that up to this point no sepoy had actually used the cartridge either in training or in the field. Some of them had only carried them around in 1855 in their pouches. As pointed out earlier, the cartridges of the Enfield Rifle was a cause of great alarm among the sepoys and was certainly a key factor in the attack perpetrated by Mangal Pandey on his white officers in Barrackpore in March 1857. But even before that the sepoys in Barrackpore had expressed their disaffection about the new cartridge. On 2 February in Barrackpore, during the evening parade of the 2nd N.I., the sepoys expressed their mistrust of the new cartridges and declared that they were suspicious of the cartridge paper as well. This meant that their fears about losing their caste would not disappear even if they used their own greasing material. In the court of inquiry that was instituted to investigate this kind of insubordinate behaviour, witness after witness spoke about their suspicions regarding the paper which they found to be very different from the old paper – 'stiff and like cloth in the mode of tearing it' as one of the sepoys explained.[28] In early February, there was a show of defiance against the new cartridges in Berhampore, a small town 120 miles upriver from Calcutta, but a full-scale mutiny and bloodshed were narrowly averted.[29] Very significantly, the official enquiry into the Berhampore incident revealed that the rumour about the cartridges had been circulating for at least two months. The British authorities had picked it up only after the taunt of the *khalasi* to the Brahmin sepoy. In the sepoy lines, the new cartridge and the loss of caste and religion had been the subjects of heated discussions.

British officers had failed to take cognizance of this disaffection even though loyal sepoys had informed them. On 6 February, for example, in Barrackpore a sepoy of the 34th N.I. (a regiment to be disbanded in April because of disloyalty) came to Captain A.S. Allen to report that a plot was being hatched among the four regiments in Barrackpore to mutiny as a protest against the attempts being made to despoil the sepoys' caste and religion and to make them Christians. The British authorities failed to take note of such information. They failed to realize how deeply these sentiments affected the sepoys. There was a lack of sympathy, a failure to understand the profound attachment of the sepoys to their caste and religion. The authorities felt that a verbal assurance to the sepoys by way of lectures and addresses would remove the fears about the government's intentions. This failure instigated fear and suspicion and drove sepoys to action.

KILL THE WHITE MAN

AN UNEASY LULL PREVAILED ALL over North India in the month of April. Officers reported the circulation of *chapattis* and of other rumours and confessed that they were utterly bewildered by all this. In April, a group of sepoys from the disbanded 19th N.I., which had been stationed in Barrackpore, arrived in Kanpur and said, according to one witness, 'We shall quarrel with the Government presently; for new cartridges prepared with cows' and pigs' fat are going to be served out, and the sepoys refuse to receive them' (Mukherjee, 1998: 47). British officers also reported about the deep unhappiness and fear in the sepoy lines about the new cartridges, which would lead to loss of caste and religion. Incendiary fires in various cantonments were signs of the growing disaffection. Officers spoke to their regiments and tried to dispel their suspicions (Kaye I: ch 6). But no one was certain that they succeeded in getting across to the sepoys or in comprehending what they intended to do. One officer warned:

> Feeling is as bad as can be and matters have gone so far that I can hardly devise any suitable remedy. We make a grand mistake in supposing that because we dress, arm and drill Hindustani soldiers as Europeans, they become one bit European in their feelings and ideas. I see them on parade for two hours daily, but what do I know of them for the other 22? What do they talk about in their lines, what do they plot? ... For all I can tell I might as well be in Siberia. I know that at the present moment an unusual agitation is pervading the ranks of the entire native army, but what it will exactly result in, I am afraid to say. I can detect the near approach of the storm ... but I can't say how, when or where it will break forth ... I don't think they know themselves what they will do, or that they have any plan of action except of resistance to invasion of their religion, and their faith. But good God! Here are all the elements of combustion at hand, 100,000 men, sullen, distrustful, fierce, with all their deepest and inmost sympathies, as well as worst passions, roused, and we thinking to cajole them into good humour by patting them on the back, saying what a fool you are for making a fuss about nothing. They no longer believe us, they have passed out of restraint and will be off at a gallop before long. If a flare-up from any cause takes place at one station, it will spread and become universal.[30]

This extraordinarily perceptive passage was written sometime in April 1857. Within a few weeks it proved to be prophetic. On 10 May, the garrison in Meerut mutinied and in a few weeks time mutiny had become 'universal' all over the Gangetic plain.

The Meerut Outbreak[31]

The mutiny in Meerut originated with a firing parade that had been ordered by Colonel Carmichael-Smyth on 24 April. It came to be known later that as soon as the order of the parade had been posted, there was a discussion in the sepoy lines. Two Muslim *naiks* (corporals), Pir Ali and Kudrat Ali told their comrades that the new cartridges were greased with the fat of cows and pigs and would defile both Hindus and Muslims. The sepoys then took an oath – Muslims on the Quran and Hindus on Ganges water – that they would not use the cartridges until every regiment had agreed to do so. (60) When the parade commenced, ninety sepoys of the 3rd Light Cavalry were asked to take the cartridges, eighty-five of them refused. This body of men, eighty-five strong, were taken off duty and confined to their lines. A court of inquiry was instituted, and approved by the Commander-in-Chief it recommended a court martial of all eighty-five sepoys.

On 9 May, the punishment of the disobedient sepoys was organized as a spectacle. All the troops, British and native, were brought on to the European infantry parade ground and were made to form three sides of a square. The European troops were fully armed but the sepoys were not. The condemned men were then marched into the square. The sentence was read out to them, they were stripped of their uniform and were then publicly ironed. The last process – the shackling of eighty-five men – took over two hours. The condemned sepoys created an outcry; they taunted the sepoys standing on the sides, and appealed to them for rescue. As they were marched off to jail, they abused their officers, especially Carmichael-Smyth at whom some of them hurled their boots. The ceremony of punishment imposed a palpable nervous strain on the native troops. (68)

The outbreak the next day was not exactly unannounced. On the evening of the same day a native officer of the 3rd Light Cavalry came to the bungalow of Lieutenant Gough, the temporary troop commander and informed him that the native troops in Meerut would mutiny the next day. He conveyed this to both Carmichael-Smyth and to Brigadier Archdale Wilson. Both of them discounted the story. The wife of the commissioner of Meerut, Mrs Greathed, told Colonel Custance of the Carabiniers that she had heard that placards had been put out in the city calling upon all true Muslims to rise and slaughter the English. Enquiries into the Meerut outbreak revealed that on the afternoon of 10 May around 2 p.m. a sepoy had told a prostitute in the Sudder Bazaar that the native troops would mutiny that day. (70) Even those who took these warnings seriously did not quite expect the ferocity of what followed.

It is difficult, of course, to pinpoint when and how the mutiny began. From all existing accounts it seems that in the late afternoon, around 5 p.m., there was an outcry in the Sudder Bazaar that European troops were coming to deprive the native regiments of their arms and ammunition. The sepoys who were in the bazaar rushed back to their lines. The sepoys of the 20th N. I. rushed forward to the bell of arms, broke it open and opened fire. They shot and killed Colonel Finnis. The 11th N.I. was also in uproar. (76) A similar scenario unfolded in the cavalry lines. There, since the sepoys had horses, the action was swifter and their destruction more far-reaching. The sepoys from the cavalry rushed from the parade ground to the jail where their comrades had been sent the previous day. The jail was broken open and the condemned sepoys freed. As a group of sepoys from the cavalry passed through the city they called on the people to join them in a war of religion.(81-82)

In both the infantry and the cavalry lines pandemonium reigned, and there was sound of gunfire all around. The lines and the bungalows were set on fire. One eyewitness recalled the scene:

> ...the lines were being burnt and there was a general rush to the magazine, where the men helped themselves to the ammunition – regardless of its being the "unclean cartridges". As for any efforts on my part to bring them to a sense of their duties or of obedience to my orders they were absolutely useless...After a time the disregard of my authority changed to open mutiny; there were loud shouts of "*Maro! Maro!*"(Kill him! Kill him!) and a few men, chiefly recruits fired pistol shots at me, mostly at random...[I] left at a gallop being for a time pursued with shouts and execrations.[32]

The mutiny did not remain one for very long. It became an outbreak as the defiance and the violence moved from the barracks to the bazaar. As the news of the mutiny of 20th N.I. spread, crowds of the ordinary people of Meerut, especially those belonging to the lower castes – 'the bazaar mobs,' according to British observers – joined the outbreak and entered the bungalow area. Plunder, arson and murder followed. The targets were clearly defined: Europeans, all that the Europeans owned and the symbols of European power. Thus the bungalows were the first to be burnt and the Europeans found in them or trying to escape were killed. Gender and age were no bar to the killings. The Old Jail, as distinct from the one that the cavalry sepoys had broken open to free their comrades, was broken and the convicts released. Sometime during the night, the mob was strengthened by bands of villagers coming in from the surrounding villages. The mutiny was poised to become a general uprising as the destruction was no longer in the hands of a disgruntled soldiery. Sepoys and the common people had merged in a single rebellion. It is easy to assume that the destruction and the violence were mindless and the plunder was the product of greed. Such an assessment overlooks one simple but significant fact: sometime during the evening, as the mayhem raged in Meerut, the rebels had cut the telegraph line to Delhi and Agra. The telegraph was of course the symbol of British rule and an alien way of life. It was also the quickest way to communicate news and to ask for reinforcements. By cutting the telegraph line, the rebels ensured that their next object of attack could not be revealed. As night fell on Meerut, a group of sepoys sped southwards to Delhi, the seat of the Mughal Emperor.

The Revolt Spreads

The sepoys from Meerut arrived at Lal Qila (Red Fort), the seat of the Mughal Emperor, Bahadur Shah II, early in the morning of 11 May. The palace was awake already as it was the month of Ramazan. Bahadur Shah was an emperor only in name. His powers had been taken away from him by the British and he lived off a pension the latter provided. He took refuge in music and poetry. Yet he enjoyed the charisma associated with the name of the Mughal Badshah.

The rebels from Meerut entered the Mughal capital through the eastern end, crossing the Yamuna by the bridge-of-boats where they killed the toll-keeper. The toll-house was set on fire and a European civilian who had driven up to the bridge was shot. Having crossed the river, the sepoys came to the eastern wall of the fort. It was here that Bahadur Shah saw them. He summoned his physician Hakim Ahsanullah Khan and told him, 'Look the cavalry are coming in by the road of the *Zer Jharokha*.' The sepoys rode up beneath the windows of the king's apartments and appealed to him, 'Dohai Badshah (Help, O King), we pray for assistance in our fight for the faith.' The powerless monarch, taken aback by this appeal, was in no position to respond and so he sent for Captain Douglas, the commandant of the palace guard. Douglas ordered the sepoys to go back. The sepoys moved off and Douglas got busy trying to close all the gates of the walled city. But he was too late. Another group of sepoys from Meerut had already entered the city and started plundering the European quarters in Daryaganj. The sepoys soon started attacking and killing any European that they saw. The 38th N.I. on guard at the palace showed its defiance by refusing to close the palace gates and by firing their guns in the courtyard of Diwan-i-Khas. This brought the king out to meet them. Ghulam Abbas, the *vakil* of the emperor, recalled the encounter:

> ...the officers of the cavalry came forward, mounted as they were, and explained that they had been required to bite cartridges, the use of which deprived both Hindus and Mahomedans of their religion, as the cartridges were greased with beef and pork fat, that they accordingly killed the Europeans at Meerut, and had come to claim his protection. The King replied, "I did not call for you, you have acted very wickedly." On this about one or two hundred of the mutinous infantry, the infantry from Meerut having also arrived by this time, ascended the steps, and came into the hall, saying, "Unless you, the King, join us, we are all dead men, and we must in that case just do what we can for ourselves." The King then seated himself in a chair, and the soldiery, officers and all, came forward one by one, bowed their heads before him, asking him to place his hand on them. The King did so, and each withdrew.[33]

An old and powerless monarch, surrounded by insurgents, reluctantly accepted the nominal leadership of the rebellion and gave it his blessing. A revolt that had begun in Meerut had acquired the sanction and stamp of authority, which was distinct from the British. It had acquired a legitimacy.

Outside the Red Fort, in the city, the insurgency had not waited for any official sanction. The mutineers joined by the common people of Delhi proceeded to plunder, to destroy and to kill. The violence was directed at all things British and at Britons. The city and its populace went over to the rebellion. The Britons who survived took refuge on the Ridge, two miles north of the city.

> **“THE REVOLT IN MEERUT DID NOT REMAIN ONE FOR VERY LONG. IT BECAME AN OUTBREAK AS THE DEFIANCE AND THE VIOLENCE MOVED FROM THE BARRACKS TO THE BAZAAR.”**

The fall of Delhi had a remarkable impact on the cantonments all over North India. Between 10 and 14 May, there were no outbreaks of violence. But once the news of the fall of Delhi had travelled down the Ganges valley, the garrisons of North India raised the flag of revolt. The fall of Delhi was interpreted as the breakdown of British authority. As early as end-May 1857, Henry Lawrence in Lucknow had perceived the importance of Delhi in the way events were unfolding. He wrote to the secretary of the Governor-General: 'Tranquility cannot be much longer maintained unless Delhi is speedily captured.'[34]

Most historians of the revolt in 1857 tend to look at the events in terms of regions and thus fail to notice any pattern in the way the mutinies spread across the

Gangetic plain. The dates of the mutinies suggest a pattern: 20 May, Aligarh; 23 May, Etawah and Mainpuri; 27 May, Etah; 30 May, Lucknow and so on down the Gangetic plains. From Lucknow, the mutinies also travel southwards to Kanpur and to Jhansi in Bundelkhand and northwards to Gonda and Bahraich on the borders of Nepal. It does seem from the dates and the places that the mutinies were spreading down the Ganges valley from Delhi with a time-gap between the various stations required for the news to travel from one place to another (Mukherjee: 1984).

The transmission of the message of mutiny from one sepoy line to another was possible because of direct communication between the sepoys of one cantonment and another. Such communication was often direct. The 7th Awadh Irregular communication of the message of rebellion, the experience of Francois Sisten, an Indian Christian police inspector in Sitapur, is worth noting. He had gone to pay his respects to the joint magistrate of Saharanpur, and was dressed and seated like an Indian. A Muslim junior district official from Bijnor entered and asked Sisten where he was from. On hearing the latter was from Awadh, he asked, 'What news from Awadh? How does the work progress brother?' Sisten replied, 'If we have work in Awadh, your highness will know it well.' The official interpreting this as caution said, 'Depend upon it, we will succeed this time, the direction of the business is in able hands.' People, it would appear, were planning and talking about the uprising. The official was later to become the principal rebel leader of Bijnor.[38]

roads and approaches to the cantonment (Mukherjee:1984: 70).

Instances of planning and co-ordination suggest the existence of decision-making bodies that discussed the plan of action. The crucial questions are what were such bodies and how and when were they formed? Tentative answers to these questions can be suggested on the basis of certain clues in the available documentation. Captain Hearsey of the Awadh Military Police in Sitapur had been given protection by his Indian subordinates during the mutiny. The 41st N.I., stationed at the same place, insisted that as they had murdered all their officers it was necessary for the police to do the same or deliver Hearsey as prisoner to the 41st N.I. The Military Police refused to do either and it was decided to settle the matter by referring it to a *panchayat*, i.e., a collective

“THE FALL OF DELHI HAD A REMARKABLE IMPACT. BETWEEN 10 AND 14 MAY, THERE WERE NO OUTBREAKS OF VIOLENCE. BUT WITH THE FALL OF DELHI, THE GARRISONS OF NORTH INDIA RAISED THE FLAG OF REVOLT.”

Infantry, who had refused to take the cartridges in early May, wrote to the 48th N.I. that 'they had acted for the faith and awaited the 48th's orders.' [35] Men moved from one sepoy barrack to another carrying the message of mutiny: Kaye called them the 'emissaries of evil' (Kaye: 2: 244). Sepoys came from Benares to Lucknow 'to corrupt the troops,' according to British officers. The sepoy lines in Faizabad were swarming with mutinous sepoys from neighbouring Azamgarh and Jaunpur. In Salon, the mutiny occurred only when mutineers from Allahabad, Sultanpur and Partapgarh had come there and 'goaded' the troops in Salon to rise.[36] Edwards, the magistrate in Budaun, noted that the 10th N.I. in Fatehgarh would mutiny depending on the movements of other mutinous corps with whom they were in daily correspondence.[37] In the context of

The mutinies also had another kind of pattern. This related to the ways the sepoys behaved when they took up arms against their white superiors. The outbreak of the mutinies was not chaotic and disorderly. On the contrary, the sepoys showed a remarkable degree of planning and coordination in their actions. In most stations, the mutinies began at a pre-appointed signal: in Bareilly, Lucknow and Meerut, for example, the signal was the firing of the evening gun; in Faizabad it was the sounding of the 10 p.m. bugle (Mukherjee:1984: 68). The execution of the mutiny was also not chaotic. In Faizabad, as the bugle sounded the troops quickly organized themselves: they stopped the gunners from touching their guns and under the direction of a native infantry officer (*risaladar*), the English officers of the station were placed with quarter guard. The cavalry patrolled all

body composed of native officers drawn from each regiment.[39] In Kanpur, *panchayats* were a nightly occurrence in sepoy lines.[40] Enquries conducted in Barrackpore after Mangal Pandey's show of defiance revealed that midnight meetings were common. There is a suggestion in all these instances that matters were discussed and decided collectively. Given the character of the sepoy lines, it is not difficult to imagine sepoys sitting together to talk about their fears and to decide their future.

The sepoys were the makers of their own rebellion: they did not challenge British rule in a fit of absent-mindedness. They were conscious agents and their acts were marked by deliberation and planning. As conscious agents the sepoys chose to destroy. Direct action informed the sepoys' moment of insurgency. In each and every station, the mutinies commenced with extensive acts of arson and plunder. The official narrative from Meerut described the ferocity of the destruction:

> the inveterate animosity with which the work of destruction was carried out … may be judged by the fact, that houses built entirely of masonry, with nothing inflammable, except the doors and beams which a considerable height from the ground supported the roof formed of cement, resting on kiln-burnt bricks, were as effectually destroyed as the thatched bungalows. Property, which the miscreants could not carry off, was thrown out and smashed into fragments, evidently pounded with heavy clubs.[41]

The destruction was not indiscriminate. Property owned, used or lived in by the British was always the first to be attacked. Thus the bungalows in which the Europeans lived were invariably the first to be attacked and burnt. Buildings identified with the British, their institutions, their symbols of power were always destroyed. The jail, the record room, the telegraph office et al., were objects of rebel wrath. In Etawah, to take a typical example, the *kachari*, the sessions court house, the post office and two bungalows went up in flames.[42] Almost always the records of the division were destroyed in a symbolic rejection of all that the foreign power had enshrined in its records. For the mutineer, the sign of enmity was unmistakable. The enmity could also be extended through association. Friends of the British became enemies of the sepoys. Thus, the Bengalis who were seen as the kin of a Christian were plundered. Bholanath Chunder, a Bengali wrote,

> The Bengalis cowered in fear, and awaited within closed doors to have their throats cut. The women raised a dolorous cry at the near prospect of death [as] from massacring their officers, and plundering the Treasury, and letting open the gaol-bird, the sipahis spread through the town to loot the inhabitants.[43]

By this logic of extension those that had gained from British rule became targets of rebel fury. Dunlop described one such attack in vivid terms:

> … many of the prisoners released had enemies in the district, mostly Bunyahs who had brought suits in our courts and the arrival of a period of anarchy was at once seized on by them to wreak a summary revenge on almost all the Bunyah caste. Thus at the village of Bhojpore, the best house, a large brick building with a courtyard in the center and massive wooden portals, belonged to the family of a Mahajun or Bunyah, by name Beharee Lall, who was a four *biswa* (or one-fifth) sharer of that village; one of the other shareholders, a Jat, was at the time of the outbreak in prison, confined for debt under the Civil court decree at the suit of the Bunyah. He arrived during the night of the 11th at Bhojpore with a few of his fellow prisoners and at daylight the villagers were collected for an attack on the Bunyah's house.[44]

What began as an individual vendetta was transformed into an entire village's fury against a perceived oppressor and led to the latter's destruction.

What accompanied the destruction was violence directed at the white man's body. The sepoys aimed to kill the white man irrespective of age and gender. 'Troopers and sipahees,' says the official narrative of the Meerut outbreak, 'were plundering, burning and destroying in every direction and savagely hunting to death every European, every Christian, man, woman or child they could find.'[45] This desire to kill had a context. It grew out of the violence that was embedded in British rule in India. British rule was based on violence since it began as an act of conquest. In the three Presidency towns of Calcutta, Bombay and Madras strategies of winning collaboration and consensus – the attempt to make the basis of rule persuasion rather than coercion and to give it a semblance of legitimacy – had been put into place through the project of social and educational reforms. But in North India, brought under the British aegis only in the nineteenth century, violence was the ultimate imprimatur of British rule. Nowhere was the inscription of this power more manifest than on the body of the sepoys who had helped the British to conquer and to expand their rule. The sepoy was recruited from the peasantry but was then given the bearing of a soldier. His life, his daily routine, his dress and even his posture was governed by a discipline imposed by the army. A breach of this discipline was severely punished, most often by flogging. A show of defiance or mutiny inevitably brought forth death by public hanging and in extreme cases by blowing from the mouth of a canon. The sepoy was treated as an inferior creature and he was abused and kicked around. The sepoy's body bore the inscriptions of subjection and violence. And when the sepoy chose, as he did in the summer of 1857, to overthrow the subjection he replicated the violence by directing it on the body of his quondam masters. Killing was the modality the sepoys chose to rid themselves of the domination of the white man.[46] The sepoys killed with a vengeance, but they did not rape. In 1858, Lord Canning ordered a complete enquiry on the dishonouring of British women by rebels in North India. The enquiry could not find a single instance of rape.[47]

The springboard of the violence was the common hatred of all things British. The hatred was aggravated by the perception shared by the sepoys that the British wanted to despoil their caste and religion. The sepoys used violence to save what was most dear to them, their dharma. The concept of dharma is a little more all embracing than religious faith. It is something that holds together life. The fear of losing dharma brought the sepoys together and drove them to act, and to act violently; dharma also served as the focus of solidarity and fraternity. Here the experience of Ranjit Singh Bissein, a former *havildar* of the 63rd N.I. is illustrative. On 24 May, he was coming into Lucknow, when he passed a police outpost:

> the police [Ranjit Singh reported] were lounging around on the charpoys. They called him to come and sit down and talk. They said they were new levies stationed there. He asked what duty was assigned to them. They said they were to oppose any of the sepoys and fight them. But they added, we shall not fight them. *Kala kala admi sab eyk hyn. Deen ke bat hyn Hum log kaye ko bedharam ho.* All black men are one. It is a matter of dharma. Why should we lose our dharma?[48]

British rule was seen as a challenge to a familiar and cherished way of life and sepoys were willing to take lives and lose their own lives in defence of their dharma.

The spread of a perceived threat on religion and the transmission of the fear, of rumours and the message of mutiny was facilitated by two factors. One was the common routine that the sepoys shared in their lines: their social life, such as it was, was confined to their lines and was determined by their caste and their religion.[49] The other was the fact that most of the sepoys of the Bengal Army came from the same background and the same area. Detailed recruitment data for the Bengal Army for the period before 1857 is not available but whatever data has been unearthed shows that the vast majority of the sepoys from the

Bengal Army came from Awadh and eastern Uttar Pradesh and belonged to upper castes.[50]

Peasants drawn from Awadh were moulded into becoming soldiers. But their social life retained aspects of their peasant background. Their peasant identity was overlaid by the uniform of the Bengal Army. News from their homes – the annexations of Lord Dalhousie, the new revenue settlements, other policy measures of the government, the rumours circulating – were discussed in the sepoy lines, and the sepoys in their turn communicated their own fears about the cartridges and the threat to their dharma. This common background and the easy communication explains why the mutinies so swiftly transformed themselves into popular insurgency. The sepoys merged with the common people from whom they had been recruited. But this return of the sepoys to their peasant origins placed them in a unique position within the rebellion which they had begun. It is necessary now to take forward the story of the revolt by looking at what happened in North India after the mutinies had struck with remarkable success and made British rule collapse, in the words of one British officer 'like a house made of cards.'[51]

REVOLT OF THE PEOPLE

THE MOST REMARKABLE FEATURE of the mutinies was the fact that hardly without exception in North India, they were followed very quickly by a rising of the civil population. In most stations, the uprisings of the sepoys merged into a civil rebellion, and this gave the revolt of 1857 its mass and overwhelming character.

The swift transformation of the mutinies into a popular uprising was noted in Meerut where it all began. The official narrative for Meerut commented:

> Before a shot was fired, the inhabitants of the Sudder Bazar went out, armed with swords, spears, clubs, any weapon they could lay hands on, collected in crowds in every lane and alley, at every outlet of the bazars; and the residents of the wretched hamlets … were to be seen similarly armed pouring out to share in what they evidently knew was going to happen.[52]

It appeared as if the common people of North India were waiting for the mutinies to initiate the uprising and they also realized the enormity of what the mutinies had achieved. One British officer wrote,

> to the mass of the population, to the poor and illiterate … it naturally seemed that the might and power of their late rulers had in truth been swept away, as it were, by one fierce blast.[53]

As the mutinies commenced, the sepoys 'divest[ed] themselves of their uniform,' tore off the regimental colours and broke out from their lines.[54] As three sepoys giving evidence before the British said, 'the men [sepoys] did as they liked. No, they did not dress in uniform.' A native Christian drummer describing life in the rebel camp narrated how the British military discipline was mocked by mimicking the stiffness of British soldiers. He also recorded that on the day of the mutiny in Kanpur, the bugler had refused to sound the assembly, one of the signals by which the sepoys' life was organized. He reiterated that the 'sepoys did just as they liked.'[55] A native officer of the Bombay Army, who had come home on leave to his village near Kanpur, reported that

> the sepoys rode on officers' and gentlemen's horses, carriages and buggies. They were not at all obedient to the native officers who went on their own ponies etc. On the contrary, the native officers were much bullied by the sepoys who did as they liked.[56]

From Meerut too, came a similar description: most of the mutineers were in undress and 'they went to Delhi not in military array, but in straggling disorder.'[57] In short, the sepoys in the moment of mutiny cast off the markers with which an alien power had sought to regiment them and thus set them apart from the peasantry from which the sepoys were recruited. Of course the one marker they would not jettison was their arms. The peasant in uniform disowned his uniform to become the peasant with arms. In eschewing the regimental discipline that the British officers had drilled into them, they reclaimed their peasant character and merged with the ordinary people.

This merging of the sepoy element into the common people is important since the sepoys, despite their peasant origins, were in a unique position. Within the domain of popular insurgency they were the only section proximate to the state power. As sons of the peasantry, they had left their villages, seen the world and now during the revolt had, as it were, brought the world back to the village. This was a rite of passage through which the peasant became initiated into the mysteries of the state: he graduated from the knowledge of mere officialdom to a knowledge of the state as the authentic object of hatred. This hatred was writ large in the selection of the rebels' targets. The return of the sepoy to the rural community as an armed peasantry was thus informed by a new consciousness.

The swift success of the mutinies and the transformation of the mutinies into a popular rebellion were noted by the British administration in Calcutta and acted upon immediately. By the beginning of June 1857, the Delhi, Meerut, Rohilkhand, Agra, Allahabad and Benares divisions had been placed under martial law. Further,

> Having first, by Act No 8 of 1857, strengthened the hands of officers by giving them greater powers for the assembling of Courts' Martial and by making the Proceedings of those Courts more summary, the Government adopted measures which should give them the services not only of their own Military and Civil officers, but of independent English gentlemen not connected with the East India Company, Indigo Planters and other Persons of intelligence and influence. These measures were as follows: On the 30th May when it was known that the mutiny of the sepoys had been followed in many places by rebellion of the populace, Act No XI of 1857 was passed. By this law persons guilty of rebellion or of waging war against the Queen or the Government, or of aiding or abetting therein, were rendered liable to the punishment of death and to the forfeiture of all their property and the crime of harbouring rebels etc. was made heavily punishable: the Supreme and Local Executive Governments were empowered to issue a Commission in any district in a state of rebellion for the trial of rebels or persons charged with any other crime against the State, or with any heinous crime against person or property. The Commissioners were empowered to act singly, and were vested with absolute and final powers of judgement … By Act No XIV of 1857 passed on 6th June, provision was made for the punishment of persons convicted of exciting mutiny or sedition in the army, the offender was rendered liable to the punishment of death and the forfeiture of all his property, and persons guilty of harbouring such offenders were made liable [to] heavy punishment. Power was also to General Courts Martial to try *all persons* whether

> amenable to the articles of war or not, charged with any offence punishable by this or the preceding Act ... By Act No XVI of 1857 all heinous offences committed in any district under Martial Law or in any district to which this Act might be extended were made punishable by death, transportation or imprisonment and by forfeiture of all property and effects ... These enormous powers ... have been extended not to military officers only but to Civil Officers and trustworthy persons not connected with the Government who under Martial Law properly so called would have had no authority.[57a]

These various Acts gave Britons the power to judge and take the lives of Indians without recourse to the due processes of law. All effective inhibitions upon the exercise of power were removed. The British found it impossible to accept that a subject population had taken arms against them and had destroyed their property and their lives. As Kaye put it,

> So it happened that whilst the first bitterness of our degradation – *the degradation of fearing those whom we had taught to fear us* – was still fresh upon our people, there came a sudden accession of stout English hearts and strong English hands, ready at once to punish and to awe. (Kaye: 2: 269; italics mine)

Lieutenant Lord Roberts, later to be made Lord, wrote that the purpose of the counter insurgency measures was to show the Indians that 'with God's help Englishmen will still be masters of India.'[57b]

The British realized that to become masters of India and to restore the awe that was due to a ruling power, it was necessary to reconquer Delhi. This did not prove to be easy. In Delhi, Bahadur Shah's acceptance of the leadership of the revolt gave to the organization of the uprising a sort of structure. The Emperor appointed his sons to positions of command in the army and sent off letters to the various rajas to march to Delhi with their troops to join the King's army in an attempt to overthrow British rule. Arrangements were made to provide the sepoys with provisions and to prevent looting. But the tensions between the popular elements of the revolt and its elite leadership were already apparent. The soldiers often did not pay heed to the orders of the Emperor and frequently spoke to him in terms and tones which had never been used before to address a Mughal Badshah (Hibbert: 271).

From the end of May, tens of thousands of sepoys had entered Delhi and had camped there. The military and political objective was to attack and take the Ridge where the British garrison had taken shelter. But the indiscipline and the lack of effective command made this a long drawn out process despite the sepoys' superiority of numbers. This situation appeared to change with the appearance of Bakht Khan from Bareilly in late June. Bakht Khan secured the full confidence of Bahadur Shah and succeeded in establishing a modicum of order among the troops but he made little progress in securing the Ridge. The mood in the Royal Palace was turning to despair even as *ghazis* and *mujahideen* collected in the city to fight and die for their faith. The rebels' lack of decisiveness in attacking the Ridge gave to the British the time to get reinforcements and to launch their attack on Delhi. The reinforcements came from Punjab and at their head was Brigadier John Nicholson.

Nicholson, even before his arrival in Delhi, had set the tone of British counter insurgency measures. He hated the sepoys and when the mutinies broke out, he wrote to Herbert Edwardes, the commissioner of Peshawar,

> Let us propose a Bill for the flaying alive, impalement, or burning of the murderers of the women and children at Delhi. The idea of simply hanging the perpetrators of such atrocities is maddening. (Hibbert: 293)

Nicholson wanted to take the law into his own hands and to inflict the most 'excruciating tortures' on the mutineers. He believed that 'the punishment of mutiny is death' and he held very few courts-martial on his way to Delhi. In the Gangetic plains, in the environs of Allahabad and Benares, on his way to Kanpur, Brigadier-General James Neill had already conducted operations based on the same principles.

"BY THE BEGINNING OF JUNE 1857, THE DELHI, MEERUT, ROHILKHAND, AGRA, ALLAHABAD AND BENARES DIVISIONS HAD BEEN PLACED UNDER MARTIAL LAW."

While Nicholson surveyed his troops and prepared for the assault on Delhi, the skirmishes between the sepoys and the British continued. These encounters were always marked by ferocity as no quarters were given on either side and no prisoners were taken. From some pieces of evidence, it is clear that the fight against the British was not being carried out by the sepoys only. British soldiers noted the presence of an ugly woman – 'the fair maid of Delhi' they mockingly called her – who came out on horseback and 'fought ... like a fiend.' A contemporary noted the frequent presence of two old withered Muslim women who Went far in advance with naked swords bitterly taunting the sepoys when they held back, calling them cowards ... These women frequently did bring cartridges to the men in the barracks and walked fearlessly in perfect showers of grape (Hibbert: 296).

Ordinary people had joined the mutineers and this had brought a different character to the uprising. It was the popular participation that made the recapture of Delhi possible only after fierce fighting. It took six days (from 14 to 20 September) of intense fighting before the British could declare that Delhi had fallen to them. Much of this fighting was in narrow lanes with houses that hid marksmen. Mutinous sepoys and ordinary rebels had become indistinguishable during the fighting.

***

This merger gave to the uprising a different dimension and added to its strength. Almost every part of what is now Uttar Pradesh (then called the United Provinces of Agra and Awadh) saw a coming together of the large sections of the population and the mutinous sepoys. In Awadh, the chief theatre of popular insurrection, this feature was most noticeable. There the transformation of the army revolt into a general uprising of the people witnessed three distinct phases. The first phase was a direct sequel to the mutinies in the districts. With the collapse of British administration in the districts the only area where British authority survived was the area around the Residency in Lucknow. The rebel forces were concentrated there in the initial phase and Lucknow was under siege from the battle of Chinhat (30 June 1857) to the first Relief of Lucknow in September 1857. The second phase lasted from the first Relief to the final fall of Lucknow in March 1858 and also had the city as the focus of the fighting. The third phase was after March 1858 when the rebels dispersed into the countryside.[58]

In each of the three phases, the participation of the civil population was the most noticeable feature. In June 1857, rebels had started moving towards Lucknow. Gubbins noted that 'the force of the mutineers ... consisted altogether of regiments stationed in the provinces.'[59] What Gubbins did not note (or perhaps did not even know at that point of time) was that some *taluqdars* and members of the *nawabi* bureaucracy had already joined the rebellion and were providing the leadership. The Raja of Mahumudabad was the first to join, providing leadership to the Sitapur rebels who fought under his *naib*, Khan Ali Khan (an ex-*chakladar* of Salon) at Chinhat. Raja Jailal Singh, the Nizam of Azamgarh, was elected mouthpiece of the soldiery and as their chief. *Taluqdars*, especially those in southern Awadh, had begun to collect men, recruit sepoys and prepare ammunition as soon as they were sure that British authority had collapsed in the districts.[60]

To the south of Lucknow, in Unao, the rebels, now indistinguishable from the rural populace, were busy putting off Havelock's advance from Kanpur into Lucknow. The British general was forced to fall back again and again because of the strength of the popular opposition. An officer noted that 'Every village is held against us, the zamindars have risen to oppose us ... We know them to be all around us in bodies of 500 or 600 independent of the regular levies.'[61]

There was a plan on the part of the British to approach Lucknow via the river Gogra but it had to be abandoned because of 'the warlike population of Oude ... swarmed by mutinous troops' was apprehended to be 'too strong'.[62] In Lucknow, most of the besiegers of the Residency were thought to be *taluqdars*' men and it was believed that 'nearly every Talooqdar except the Raja of Balrampoor and Man Singh have sent his contingent to assist in the siege.'[63]

Finding themselves in a vulnerable position inside the Residency, with their supply lines cut off, the British attempted to negotiate with the rebels. But every overture made by Outram to the influential citizens of Lucknow was spurned.[64] Even after November, the native population refused to co-operate in any way with the British. Like Outram before him, Campbell also

> did his utmost to open communications with the Chiefs and Nobles and other influential inhabitants who might be well-disposed towards us. With this object he issued proclamations declaring that all people who had taken no part in the disturbances would be treated with every consideration by the British government. Such persons were invited to come and have an interview with the CC and shopkeepers and artisans were also assured that they would be treated with kindness and receive own prices for their goods ... Not a seer of provisions could be obtained nor did a man attempt to open communication with us.[65]

This was an indication of how wide the base of the rebellion was and the extent of popular support. Neither blandishments nor implied threats had any impact on the people.

Around October 1857, twelve infantry and three cavalry regiments were reported to be fighting in Lucknow. More importantly, they were reinforced by *taluqdars* and their men – 'almost all the Oude Talookdars sent men and agents.'[66] Man Singh, Hanwant Singh, Bishwanath Baksh, the son of Sangram Singh of Allahabad, the Raja of Amethi and Davi Buksh were the principal *taluqdars* fighting in Lucknow.[67] Rana Beni Madho

> **“IN DELHI, BAHADUR SHAH ZAFAR'S ACCEPTANCE OF THE LEADERSHIP OF THE REVOLT GAVE TO THE ORGANIZATION OF THE UPRISING A SORT OF STRUCTURE.”**

with 2,000 men, Raghunath Singh of Khajurgaon with 2000 men, Bishon Singh of Simerpaha with 1,000 men, Bhagwan Baksh of Nain with 1000, and Sahajram of Pakhramow with 1,000 men were also entrenched in the city.[68] In November, during Campbell's relief of Lucknow, the city had 7,950 sepoys, 5,600 men of the Awadh regiments, 7,720 cavalry and 32,080 *taluqdars*' men fighting against the British forces.[69] The numbers suggest that the rebellion in Awadh had transcended a purely sepoy base. For one thing the fighting force was quite large and for another more than 60 per cent of the fighting force was drawn from the rural populace. It is more than probable, given the ties of loyalty that existed in the rural world of Awadh that the thousands of men supplied by the *taluqdars* were not all their retainers but also drawn from tenants, peasants and clansmen who lived on their land. It is significant that this report about the number of rebels ended with the words 'which numbers are being daily reinforced.'

After the evacuation of the British from Lucknow, 'crowds of people [began] flocking into the capital from the districts to take part in the struggle.'[70] By January, Lucknow was 'swarming with fighting men' and efforts were mounted to fortify the city against an expected British attack.[71] The popular base of the revolt is evident from the deliberate withholding of provisions from the British by merchants and shopkeepers. No grain dealers or vegetable vendors came forward even though extravagant prices were offered. Forays into villages were no more successful because the villagers were unwilling to part with their grain:

> The surrounding villagers still withhold every description of supplies ... Yesterday a strong forage party was sent out to Mhow, a village 11 Villages (sic) off. It was necessary to go so great a distance because The enemy had previously removed all the supplies from the intervening villages. They will now doubtless take away or conceal grain and other means of subsistence ... and our chances of obtaining supplies by foraging will consequently grow daily more precarious.[72]

Another report noted that 'everyone from the raja to the pasee is afraid to make any the slightest demonstration in our favour.'[73] Armed resistance had been reinforced by non-cooperation.

Throughout September and October of 1857, the Awadh districts served as 'feeder lines' for the fighting in Lucknow. Men were coming in to join the fight and levies were being raised.[74] In November, during the critical days of fighting against Campbell's army in Lucknow, reinforcements were 'pouring in from the districts' and even in January there were reports of 'levies ... daily being raised.'[75] Even when levies raised in the countryside were not sent direct to Lucknow, there was a certain preparedness in the districts to help the rebel cause whenever required. Orders were sent to all *taluqdars* in southern Awadh, for example, to join forces and stop the British advance. The key figure in southern Awadh for organizing rebel forces was Mehndi Hussain, the Nazim of Sultanpur. He had with him at Hussainpur, near Sultanpur, a force of 8,000 to 10,000 men and had the support of all the *taluqdars* of Sultanpur and Faizabad except Rustam Shah.[76] With Mehndi Hussain were small magnates who could provide only a few hundred men. These magnates did not move to Lucknow but remained in the districts armed and ready to scour the Awadh frontier to prevent any British advance from Allahabad or Jaunpur. With Hussain were 400 members of the Bachgoti clan. Their presence indicates that perhaps in the Awadh countryside there were leaderless bands of clansmen who had joined the fight without waiting for the local magnate or clan leaders to provide the leadership.[77] Among Mehndi Hussain's own men there were common villagers.[78]

After the fall of Lucknow, the British failed to cut off the escape routes so that the insurgents swarmed into the countryside.[79] William Howard Russell of *The Times*, London, noted in his diary on 3 April 1858:

> At present all Oudh may be regarded as an enemy's country, for there are very few chiefs who do not still hold out, and defy the threats of the Proclamation.[80]

The rebels too were conscious of both the strengths and weaknesses of their position. They knew it was no longer possible to defeat the British in one head-on confrontation. Khan Bahadur Khan, the leader of the rebellion in Rohilkhand who had moved into Awadh formulated a new strategy for the rebels:

> Do not attempt to meet the regular columns of the infidels because they are superior to you in discipline and bunderbust, and have big guns; but watch their movements, guard all the ghauts on the rivers, intercept their communications, stop their supplies, cut up their daks and posts, and keep constantly hanging about their camps; give them no rest.[81]

The new strategy was to harass the British in every possible way and not allow their administration and authority to settle down. Khan Bahadur Khan's advice was taken, for it was noted in June: 'The policy of the rebels has clearly been to harass and drive in all our *thanahs* and outposts avoiding as much as possible close contact with any disciplined troops.'[82]

Resistance was not restricted to large *taluqdars*. Even 10 or 15 miles out of Lucknow small zamindars were setting up fortifications and entrenchments with the strength of a few hundreds of men and four to five guns.[83] All *taluqdars* were not easily defeated. Narpat Singh with 22 guns inside his extremely strong fort in Reoya surprised Walpole's force with his resistance. He escaped with his men and lived to fight again. This emboldened other *taluqdars*. Drigbijai Singh followed up by sacking the British *thana* at Mahona and Loni Singh prepared himself to fight with 12,000 men in his fort at Mithauli.[84]

There existed a few *taluqdars* who were willing to tender their allegiance to the British. In April 1858, there were only 27 *taluqdars* who had sent in their allegiance either in person, through a *vakil* or in writing.[85] The rebels' attitude towards *taluqdars* who showed their loyalty to the British was one of sheer vengeance. They sought to pressurize them or to destroy their wealth. Begum Hazrat Mahal confiscated Man Singh's estate and settled it with other claimants. Man Singh pleaded for British help but this was not forthcoming since the British were in no position to enter Faizabad. The rebels besieged him in his fort and pressed him to sue for terms. The Raja of Tiloi was similarly invested by the rebels for twenty-six days and the British were unable to help their loyal ally.[86]

This turning upon loyal *taluqdars* by the rebels was a symptom of disarray, of a growing awareness among the rebels that, faced against a superior well-organized military force, their side was falling apart. But the rebellion still mustered considerable strength of numbers and maintained large though dispersed pockets of resistance. These enclaves were concentrated in the south and south-east of Lucknow, roughly corresponding to the districts of Unao, Rae Barelli, Sultanpur, Partapgarh and Faizabad; west and north-west of Lucknow in what is now Muhamadi and Sitapur and in the far-flung north in Gonda-Bahraich.[87]

Once the British crackdown under Lord Clyde began in the middle of October, things moved swiftly and the popular resistance crumbled. But this suppression of the rebellion was not without serious encounters with the rebels. Those leaders who escaped to Nepal had with them 8000 men.[88] The people of Awadh had fought the British. This is clear from the number of ordinary and common weapons that were recovered or surrendered. By the beginning of February 1859 there had been collected 29,941 spears, 427, 932 swords and 129,414 firearms.[89] Bows and arrows were counted at 6418.[90] Firearms could be recovered from the house of an ordinary peasant.[91] The total strength, in numbers, behind the rebellion is impossible to determine. According to official British estimates:

> the approximate number of rebels who have taken advantage of the Amnesty and returned to their homes without reporting themselves is according to reports received from District officers Twenty thousand one hundred and twenty. I am however directed to observe that no reliance is to be placed on this return, as the number is quite inadequate 200,000 is more likely to represent the number who have actually come in. But it would be impossible to do more than guess the numbers that have returned to their homes under the Amnesty. Probably three fourths of the adult male population of Oudh, had been in rebellion.[92]

Nothing more need be said about the participation of the ordinary people in the revolt in Awadh.

***

The other theatre of popular insurrection was Bundelkhand, especially the area around Jhansi.[93] Here the district of Banda was the first to witness a widespread rural *jacquerie*. After the released prisoners of Allahabad and Kanpur crossed into the region, villages in *parganas* Buberoo and Mow on the Jamuna rose up in rebellion. In the north of the district, *tahsils* rose one after another in early June 1857. One British officer wrote, 'The whole District went to the bad in less than a week.' The rest of the district in the west and south-west awaited the departure of the British officials from Banda before taking to arms. Tapti Roy writes, 'The sparking off of the rebellion was thus contingent upon two sets of knowledge, the first about the adversary and the second about the perceived vulnerability of that adversary.'[94]

The actions of the rebels were directed against all forms of British authority. It also extended to all features of the rural world, which were seen as products of the British intervention. Those perceived to be responsible for such features were eliminated. The nature and intensity of this popular insurgency is clear from the following description penned by a British officer:

> Tulwars and matchlocks were scarce in Bundelkhand, but armed with spears and scythes, and iron-bound lathies, and extemporary axes, formed of chopping knives fastened on sticks, they imagined to be warriors, chose their own kings, and defied all comers. Never was revolution more rapid – never more complete.[95]

The actions of the rebels were thus marked by a certain political consciousness which had the vision of an alternate order. This consciousness was evident also from the verbal insults to which the British were exposed from the rural population – a sure sign of the overturning of the structures of domination and subordination. British officers fleeing the area noticed how everywhere the villagers were armed and hostile. The rebellious spirit that gripped the people often articulated itself in symbolic acts. One officer of the 12th N.I. described how

> One man, standing almost naked on a raised platform, drew his sword and held it up aloft as we passed, in a very fine attitude. He was quite a study for a painter. It was an admirable declaration on the nation having drawn the sword to free themselves. I had no idea a Hindoostanee could assume so grand an attitude.[96]

The rebellion of the common people was complemented and strengthened in Bundelkhand by the actions of *thakurs*, the landholding magnates of the region. It was only in the beginning of 1,858 that the thakurs began rallying round to the cause of the rebels. Behind this was the growing fear of British power returning to Bundelkhand. The *thakurs* assembled in Chanderi to support the Rajas of Banpur and Shahgarh. The *thakurs* took oaths to support the Bundela chief of Banpur against the British and to fight till the end. But the *thakurs* were defeated in Lalitpur and Chanderi, and moved to Jhansi. Before the battle of Jhansi, the town had 7,000 rebels in it. Of these 1,500 were soldiers and the rest were *thakurs* and their retainers.[97]

The victory of Hugh Rose in Chanderi did not mean the end of resistance there. Once the British troops departed, the thakurs took to arms again. On 11 May the *thana* at Lalitpur was attacked and all the policemen killed. The *thana* at Bansi was captured. The fort at Chanderi was stormed and Scindia's troops driven out. In Jhansi, in the middle of May, the *thakurs* gathered in the region between Kalpi and Jhansi. The town of Mote was attacked and plundered and all the officials were plundered. British counter insurgency was matched by *thakur* resistance.[98] *Thakur* resistance posed a formidable challenge to the establishment of British authority and lingered on in the form of banditry.[99] Overlaid on the rebellion of the *thakurs* and the common people was the resistance offered by the local potentates of Bundelkhand. Among these, the important ones were Rani Lakshmibai of Jhansi, Mardan Singh of Banpur, Nawab Ali Bahadur of Banda and Kesho Rao of Gurserai.

In Jhansi, Lakshmibai was unconnected with the mutiny of the sepoys. After the mutiny the soldiers demanded guns, assistance and supplies. The British, who had taken shelter in the first, also sent messages to the Rani to come to their assistance. She wrote to the Deputy Collector, F.D.Gordon, that she had sent guns and men to the rebels to protect herself. The pressure of the rebels around her mounted and they threatened to kill her if she provided assistance to the British. On the third day of the revolt, the rebels warned the Rani that if she did not support them they would kill her. Lakshmibai provided them with reinforcements of 1,000 men and two heavy guns. Her position of neutrality was rendered untenable as her own soldiers and retainers joined the uprising. Even her personal guards went over to the rebels. Her men participated in the killing of the British. Under these circumstances, the options open to the Rani were limited: she was a reluctant rebel. An alternative version is available in the narrative of Vishnubhatt Godse who was present in Jhansi in the summer of 1857. Godse wrote, the soldiers after their mutiny went to Lakshmibai whom they considered their ruler, greeted her and said, 'We will obey your orders and receive our salary every month from you.'[100]

The Raja of Banpur, Mardan Singh, came to Lalitpur at the invitation of the deputy superintendent of Chanderi, to help in quelling the disaffection of the *thakurs* of the area. Mardan Singh did not commit any overt act of rebellion and offered his assistance to the British. When the British were forced to leave the district, they issued a *parwana* by which Mardan Singh was made in charge of the district. The British suspected him of playing a double game. But as Roy points out, this role was somewhat thrust upon him: as a leading member of the Bundela clan, 'he symbolized a power which at this point of time could be identified with the forces of rebellion while as the ruler of an independent principality he was the only one eligible to replace and overthrown British administration.'[101]

In Banda too, the British sought protection from the Nawab as soon as the first signs of danger were manifest. British women were sent to his palace and shortly after the men too took refuge there. Whatever the Nawab's intentions, it was clear that his followers did not like the presence of foreigners in the palace. Despite this opposition, the British believed that Ali Bahadur had behaved 'correctly' towards them and left the district in his charge when they withdrew.[102]

When British authority in Jalaun was on the verge of collapse, the British Deputy Commissioner asked Kesho Rai to come to his assistance and help keep the district under control. Kesho Rai was willing to provide assistance if the request came to him in writing. The Deputy Commissioner then wrote him a letter. Armed with this Kesho Rai threw out all officials and declared himself the Governor of the district. Unable to control events, the British evacuated the district.[103]

The withdrawal of British authorities from large parts of Bundelkhand created a new political situation for the potentates of the area. The absence of the British created a space for them to reassert their old power and influence but the presence of rebels all around them severely curtailed their independence. In Jhansi, effective government remained a contentious issue with no agreement emerging between the Rani and the sepoys. The latter wanted to set up Sadashiv Rao Narain, a relative to the late Raja and a claimant to the throne, as a rival to the Rani. The sepoys also proclaimed that 'The people are God's, the country is the badshah's and the two religions govern.' They demanded Rs 1,25,000 from Lakshmibai as price for the throne. Some understanding was probably arrived at for the Rani gave them Rs 15,000 and they left Jhansi on 11 June. The Rani then issued a second proclamation to the effect that the 'Raj is Lachmee Bai' and her own flag now fluttered on the fort. She enlisted 100 armed men from the local inhabitants who joined the 80 men who had deserted from Scindia's force, 300 *vilayatis*, 500 mutineers and 500 Bundela cavalry soldiers. Zamindars also sent in their quota of men. Altogether, there were about 30,000 men at the service of the Rani.[104]

On 12 and 14 June, Lakshmibai wrote to W.C. Erskine, the Commissioner and Agent to the Lieutenant-Governor in the Sagar divisions. In the first letter she wrote of her utter helplessness in the face of mutiny and popular insurgency. She affirmed her total dependence on the British and said that she had assumed the responsibility of governing Jhansi for the protection and welfare of the people. In the second, she admitted that it was becoming impossible for her to maintain law and order and pleaded for quick reinforcements. In his reply, Erskine asked the Rani to govern Jhansi on behalf of the British till such time a new superintendent arrived to take charge. She was also asked to collect revenue, raise a police force and to take steps that would have the approval of the British. She was promised reimbursement of all her expenses and a liberal deal. The letter went with an official proclamation in Hindi and Persian. The proclamation announced that the Rani was ruling Jhansi on behalf of the British and asked the people to obey her orders and to pay her revenue. The Rani also wrote to the ruler of Datia saying that all the chiefs should get together 'to check the disturbances.' Lakshmibai, contrary to popular myth, was not a willing and an immediate rebel. She proceeded with caution and was unwilling for a long time to sever her links with the British.[105]

The Raja of Banpur, Mardan Singh, took possession of Lalitpur sub-division and removed all government *thanas* and replaced them with his own people. He plundered all those who had supported the British. In Banda, British rule ended when the Nawab issued a proclamation on 14 June announcing '*Khalq khoda ki, mulk badshah ka, hukum Nawab bahadur ka*.' But this did not meet the approval of the sepoys who issued a counter proclamation, which said that the rule was that of the *subahdar* sepoy *bahadur*. The Nawab had to accept the authority of the soldiers as long as they remained in Banda. After their departure on 19 June, Ali Bahadur established his own administration. Kesho Rao in Jalaun followed his counterparts and set up his own rule.[106] There was an obvious contradiction between the sepoy element of the rebellion and the princes who sought to lead it. Roy's summing up of this situation is worth quoting: 'The rajas did not think their new authority stemmed from the mutiny; on the contrary, they looked upon themselves as natural successors of the British.'[107]

> **"THE REBELLION OF THE COMMON PEOPLE WAS COMPLEMENTED AND STRENGTHENED IN BUNDELKHAND BY THE ACTIONS OF THAKURS, THE LANDLORDS OF THE REGION."**

This contradiction, and especially the fact that mutineers were passing through Bundelkhand, restricted the freedom of the rajas. They had to contend with the power and the influence of the sepoys. Often the sepoys acted decisively and had the orders of the rulers rescinded. The other factor was the fear of an imminent return of the British, and this made rajas like Mardan Singh of Banpur attempt a united front of the chiefs and their troops against the inevitable British reconquest of Bundelkhand. Jhansi emerged as a principal target of the counter insurgency force under Hugh Rose and also of rebel action and bands of rebels congregated there. Lakshmibai made a last attempt at reconciliation but when that brought forth no response from the British, she decided to defend her beloved Jhansi. Guns were placed on the walls of the city and the houses near the walls were evacuated to house the soldiers. Rose opened fire on Jhansi on 28 March 1858 and stormed it on 3 April. After two days of fighting, he had taken over the city but the Rani had fled. There was another encounter with Rose's troops near Kalpi (22-23 May) and another in Gwalior which was Lakshmibai's swan song.[108]

***

A short-lived but an important theatre of popular insurrection was Kanpur. In fact, spelt as Cawnpore in the nineteenth century by the British, the place has come to epitomize the violence of the rebellion on both sides of the divide. In Kanpur, the mutiny of the troops was followed by a plunder of the rich and the wealthy. The city was full of villagers from the surrounding areas and they with the sepoys went around the town looting and insulting the rich (Mukherjee: 1998: 54-62). The Britons had all taken shelter in the entrenchment that General Wheeler had built. A deputation of the rebels went off to meet Nana Sahib, the heir of the Peshwa. There are two versions of this meeting. According to one version, the rebels told Nana Sahib, 'Maharaj, a kingdom awaits you if you join our cause but death if you side with our enemies.' And the Nana replied, 'What have I to do with the British? I am altogether yours.' In a royal gesture he placed his hands on the heads of the rebels and swore to join them. The other version states that when the Nana saw that the entire soldiery had completely thrown off their allegiance to the Company, he decided to join and advise them (Mukherjee: 1998: 62-63). This acceptance of leadership was significant. It gave to the revolt in Kanpur a legitimacy. The insurrection became an open and public affair, and Nana Sahib could openly inform General Wheeler that the attack on the entrenchment was about to commence. It was like a declaration of war.

“IN JHANSI, THE REBELLING SEPOYS PROCLAIMED 'THE PEOPLE ARE GOD'S, THE COUNTRY IS THE BADSHAH'S AND THE TWO RELIGIONS GOVERN'.”

The bombardment of the entrenchment lasted from 6 to 25 June. The defence of the entrenchment is one of those feats of heroism and endurance of which legends are made. Unable to defeat the British, Nana Sahib offered General Wheeler terms of a safe transit down the river to Allahabad. The British left the entrenchment on 27 June to board the boats that had been provided for them. There was a crowd of 10,000 to 12,000 people watching the British leave from Satichaura Ghat. When the last Briton had boarded, at a signal guns placed on both banks of the river, opened fire. The boatmen set fire to the thatched roofs of the boats and fled. As the screaming men, women and children jumped into the water, the cavalry went in slashing at them with their swords. The massacre was a public spectacle in which only a very few survived. All available evidence suggests that it was well planned and well executed. The decision to lure the British out of the entrenchment and then to kill them was decided in a full council of war attended by Nana Sahib, his lieutenants like Azimullah, rebels like Teeka Singh and also by Maulavi Liaqat Ali. A Hindu prince and a Maulavi sanctioned the massacre. A Qazi also declared such a massacre to be 'lawful and proper' (Mukherjee:1998: 70-75).

In Kanpur, the massacre was celebrated as great victory. Gun salutes were fired; the city was illuminated and Nana Sahib took his place on the throne (Mukherjee: 1998:75). There was, however, a second massacre in Kanpur. From those who had survived the slaughter at Satichaura, the men were separated and shot. The women and children were imprisoned in a room known as the Bibighur. As the fall of Kanpur to the British forces coming up from Allahabad became a certainty, it was decided to kill the women and children kept in the Bibighur. The sepoys were asked to kill them but they refused. Four or five professional executioners were then sent in to do the killing. The bodies – and some, it was said, were not even dead – were thrown into a well. If the massacre on the river had been a public affair, the slaughter in the Bibighur was carried out in secret. The Bibighur killings did not enjoy the sanction of a collective (Mukherjee: 1998: 78-81). The Bibighur massacre, contrary to the one in Satichaura Ghat, was perpetrated out of fear.

Without in any way underestimating the horror of the two massacres in Kanpur, they must be placed in a particular context. This relates to the counter insurgency measures used by James Neill as he advanced towards Kanpur from Allahabad. The extraordinary powers given to Britons under the various pieces of legislation discussed at the beginning of this chapter made the death sentence, on the slightest suspicion, the order of the day. Anything from rebellion, to stealing, to desertion, to possessing money for which the accused could not provide any explanation were punished by death.[109] Indiscriminate use of the death sentence was an intrinsic part of the policy that Neill adopted to 'settle' the town of Allahabad and the areas around it. According to Kaye, Neill's orders were that

> all the men inhabiting them [certain villages] were to be slaughtered. All sepoys of mutinous regiments not giving a good account of themselves were to be hanged. The town of Futtehpore which had revolted was to be attacked, and the Pathan quarters destroyed, with all their inhabitants. (Kaye: ii: 275)

The correspondent of *The Times*, William Howard Russell who was in India in early 1858 met an officer who had been part of the column that Neill sent up from Allahabad to Kanpur. The officer reported in Russell's words, that 'In two days forty-two men were hanged on the roadside, and a batch of twelve men were executed because their faces were "turned the wrong way" when they were met on the march' (Russell: 281-82). Even boys who had playfully flaunted rebel colours and had beaten a tomtom were not spared (Kaye: ii: 236). One official, in a letter to the *Daily News*, provided a graphic description of Neill's operations:

> Every native that appeared in sight was shot down without question; and in the morning Colonel Neill sent out parties of his regiment ... and burned all the villages near where the ruins of our bungalows stood, and hung every native that they could catch, on the trees that lined the road. Another party of soldiers penetrated into the native city and set fire to it, whilst volley of grape and canister was poured into the fugitives as they fled from their burning houses.[110]

The returns that the Special Commissioners submitted were most often very inadequate indicators of the number of persons tried and sentenced to death since ordinary white men had been given unprecedented powers and, according to Kaye, 'Volunteer hanging parties went out into the districts and amateur executioners were not wanting to the occasion' (Kaye: ii: 236). Subsequently, the government had to admit that 'Capital punishment was inflicted for trivial offences.'[111] Neill's forces did not just kill; they also burnt villages on an extensive scale (Mukherjee: 1998:30-31). These acts of arson were deliberate and exemplary. They aimed to destroy the rebels' self-identity. A village is the primary site of the solidarity of a community, it provides people with a sense of belonging. By burning villages, the British destroyed homesteads and human shelter, they interrupted the cycle of agriculture by burning barns and fields. Villages are also the locus of stories, myths and histories: by burning them the British sought to eradicate a culture.

Reflecting on the severity of the British counter insurgency measures, Kaye wrote,

> Over the whole of the Sepoy War there is no darker cloud than that which gathered over Allahabad in this terrible summer ... It is on the records of our British Parliament, in papers sent home by the Governor-General of India in Council, that "the aged, women and children, are sacrificed, as well as those guilty of rebellion". They were not deliberately hanged, but burnt to death in their villages ... Englishmen did not hesitate to boast or to record their boastings in writing that they had "spared no one" and that "peppering away at niggers" was a very pleasant pastime. (Kaye: ii: 269-70)

What is important to remember is the fact that the British committed these atrocities before the rebels had carried out the massacre in Kanpur. As Russell noted, 'These "severities" could not have been justified by the Cawnpore massacre, because they took place before the diabolical act' (Russell: 282). There are no reasons to believe that the rebels in Kanpur were ignorant of these British atrocities.

Neill's directives acquired a new ferocity once he entered Kanpur and learnt about the massacre on the river and discovered the Bibighur and the well. There was the thirst for revenge but Neill's directives went beyond revenge. He spelt out his method of inflicting a punishment thus: 'Whenever a rebel is caught he is sentenced to be hanged at once; but the chief rebels or ringleaders I first make clean up a certain portion of the pool of blood. To touch blood is most abhorrent to the high caste natives, they think by doing so they doom their souls to perdition. Let them think so.' Neill not only made his victims clean the blood that was spattered on the floor and the walls of Bibighur, he also gave orders that after the hangings 'all the Brahmins will be buried and all the Mahomedans burned' (Mukherjee: 1998: 32-33). Neill thus pursued his victims beyond their death by desecrating their corpses. Considered sacred and belonging to a wider community, a corpse's defilement thus affected the entire kinship network and tainted it for generations to come. Neill recognized this when he declared that he wanted to 'doom their souls to perdition.' He defiled the rebels by making them an agent of cleaning. He also transgressed the proper funerary rites of Hindus and Muslims. This not only condemned the dead man's soul but also his kin who lived after him which in rural India meant an entire community. Neill thus inflicted a post-mortem punishment on the entire community by desecrating the funerary rites. His retribution pursued the victims beyond life. By deliberately choosing a whole series of rituals and beliefs that involved entire communities, Neill recognized the collective nature of the rebellion that confronted British power. Again, by reversing in his punishments the funerary customs of Hindus and Muslims, Neill pointed to the fact that both Hindus and Muslims had been equally active in opposing British rule. The retributive violence of the British was total: it attacked an entire culture. By their very totality, the counter-insurgency measures recognized the nature of the opposition. An opposition that had been active in destroying all aspects of the British presence could only be taught an exemplary lesson by a violence that was total.

WAR OF RELIGION AND RESTORATION

THE BRITISH TOOK NEARLY ONE year to restore their authority over the areas which had been affected by the rebellion of 1857. It is important to understand what held the rebellion together for such a long time and over such an extensive area. An earlier section argued that the mutinies and the revolt grew out of a desire to protect dharma. It was driven by a fear that the British were pursuing a deliberate policy to despoil caste and religion. More than the reality, the perception of the people was crucial in this matter. The uprising drew its strength also from this same fear. The battle to overthrow British rule was fought out as a war of religion. Defence of religion was the rebellion's rallying cry.

This aspect of the uprising becomes clear from the *ishtahars* or proclamations that the rebel leadership issued to rally the people and to maintain the unity and the momentum of the revolt. If religion was one side of the proclamations, the other side was their virulent anti-British character. One proclamation issued during the early phase of the revolt abused the British and their reigning monarch, Queen Victoria, and urged the people to fight the British in every possible way.[112] But it was the defence of religion which was the dominant theme of most proclamations. The rebels believed, without exception, that the British (in the words of one *ishtahar*) 'wish to deprive the Hindoos and Mahomedans of their religion and wish them to become Christians.'[113] A Mughal prince Feroze Shah informed the people that 'within the last few years the British commenced to oppress the people in India, under different pleas and continued to eradicate Hindooism and Mahomedanism and to make all the people embrace Christianity.' He circulated a list of the 'real intentions' of the British and these were: (1) burning all the books of every other religion, (2) making eating and drinking with Europeans compulsory for Indians seeking employment, (3) destroying mosques and temples, (4) forbidding Maulavis and Brahmins to preach, (5) administering all law courts according to English law, (6) compelling all marriages to take place according to English customs under the supervision of English priests, (7) prohibiting all prescriptions made out by Hindu and Muslim physicians and substituting these with English medicine, (8) disallowing Hindu and Muslim fakirs from converting people without the permission of Christian missionaries, and (9) allowing only European doctors to assist Indian women during childbirth. The most sensitive issues were deliberately picked out to instigate the people and to show that 'the real purpose of this war is to save religion.'[114] In another version of the same proclamation, Feroze Shah saw himself as God's servant and his resistance to British rule as 'doing God's work.'[115] A party of prisoners was individually asked before their execution why they had fought and what was the object of the war. And each one of them replied: 'The slaughter of the English was required by our religion.'[116]

A group of sepoys while retreating into Nepal offered an explanation for their actions and hoped this would act as a plea for mercy. They wrote

> For a century ago the British arrived in Hindoostan and gradually entertained troops in their service, and became masters of every state. Our forefathers have always served them and we also entered their service. By the mercy of God and with our assistance the British also conquered every place they liked, in which thousands of us, Hindoostani men were sacrificed, but we never made any excuses or pretences nor revolted ... But in the year 1857 the British issued an order that new cartridges and muskets which had arrived from England were to be issued in the former of which the fats of cows and pigs were mixed; and also the attah of wheat mixed with powdered human bones was to be eaten; and even distributed them in every Regiment of infantry, cavalry and artillery ... They gave these new cartridges to the sowars of the 3rd Light Cavalry, and ordered them to bite them; the troopers objected to it, and said that they would never bite them; for if they did, their religion and faith would be destroyed ... Upon this the British officers paraded the men of the three regiments and having prepared 1400 English soldiers, and other battalions of European troops and Horse Artillery, surrounded them, and placing 6 guns before each of the infantry regiments, loaded the guns with grape and made 84 new troopers prisoners and put them in jail with irons on them ... The reason, that the sowars of the said Cantonment were put into jail, was that we should be frightened into biting the new cartridges; on this account we and all our countrymen having united together, have ... fought with the British for the preservation of our faith ... we have been compelled to make war for two years and the Rajahs who are with us in faith and religion, are still so, ... we have fought for two years in order that our faith and religion may not be polluted. If the religion of a Hindoo or Mussalman is lost, what remains in the world.[117]

The insurgents saw the revolt as a war of religion. This, much to the surprise of the British did not create any divisions. The authorities authorized an expenditure of Rs 50,000 to help raise the Hindu population of Bareilly against the Muslim rebels. But the attempt failed (Mukherjee: 1984: 153-54). One reason for the absence of division on the basis of religion was the fact that the revolt was seen as a war in which both Hindus and Muslims had equally to lose or gain. In the various proclamations Hindu-Muslim co-existence within the Mughal imperial framework was always emphasized. Bahadur Shah's proclamation declared:

> I, who am the grandson of Abul Muzuffer Serajuddin Bahaudr Shah Ghazee, King of India, having in the course of circuit come here to extirpate the infidels ... and to liberate and protect the poor helpless people now groaning under their iron rule, have by the aid of the Majahdeens, or religious fanatics, erected the standard of Mohammad, and persuaded the orthodox Hindoos who had been subject to my ancestors, and have been and are still accessories in the destruction of the English, to raise the standard of Mahavir.[118]

A pamphlet called *Fateh Islam* (Victory of Islam) spoke of the Hindus and Muslims as 'brethren to each other.' It asked the Hindus to join the fight to 'butcher the English' and added, 'The Hindoos will remain steadfast to their religion, while we will also retain ours. Aid and protection will be offered by us to each other' (Mukherjee: 1984: 153). This unity was not merely tactical and politic. It carried with it the stamp of spontaneity and it harked back to the Mughal traditions with which the rebels identified. This spirit of harmony was expressed in Lucknow in the early days of the uprising when rebels called the young prince Birjis Qadr from the palace and hailed him as Kanhaiya (Lord Krishna) (Mukherjee: 1984: 87).

There was one aspect of the war of religion that needs to be noted because of its uniqueness. Through the summer of 1857 and later, a very large section of Indian society was in open war with a power, which it considered to be alien, interfering and hostile. In many places, the rebels had British women at their mercy. They killed the women but did not rape them. But in England and among Britons in India, there was a widespread belief that women had been dishonoured. In 1858, Lord Canning ordered an enquiry on the dishonouring of British women by the rebels all over North India. The findings of the enquiry were unambiguous:

> nothing has come to my knowledge which would in the smallest degree support any of the tales of dishonour current in our public prints. Direct evidence, wherever procurable, has been steadily and consistent against them. The people, those who must know had there been cases of outraged honour and would have told us, uniformly deny that such things were ever perpetrated or thought of.

District officers from all over North India wrote in to say that they had found no evidence of dishonour to women. It is important to explain this absence of rape. Even in Kanpur, where in the Bibighur, the rebels had British women at their mercy for fifteen days, there was no rape. Lieutenant Colonel Williams, who conducted the investigations into the massacres in Kanpur concluded, 'the most searching and earnest enquiries totally disprove the unfounded assertion that was at first so frequently made, and so currently believed, that personal indignity and dishonour had been offered to our poor suffering country women.' I would suggest two possible explanations. I have argued that the rebellion of 1857 saw itself as a struggle to preserve the purity of caste and religion of both Hindus and Muslims against a perceived attempt by the British to interfere with the social customs and beliefs of the people. The fight to maintain purity went so far as to label all loyalists as Christians. It was said that in conversation among rebels the British were never mentioned, for 'a man's mouth became impure [for] forty days by naming the *kafirs*.' In such a situation, sexual contact with British women would obviously be considered or child who fell into their hands.' Where the desire to kill and destroy was overwhelming, rape was seen as redundant.

But this analysis is not without problems. Most of the women who had fallen into the hands of the rebels had been killed. Thus when the enquiry was conducted there was no way of knowing from them what had been inflicted upon their bodies before they were killed. It is also easy to imagine that British women who had escaped being killed would not be too eager to speak of their experiences, if they had been raped. Rape victims are always reticent because of the utter humiliation, violation and social stigma that rape involves. No enquiry can sufficiently probe the world of such a

> Mussulmans nor Hindoos – nay, not even Jews, sun worshippers, or fire worshippers can believe it true. To eat pigs and drink wine, to bite greased cartridges, and to mix pigs fat with flour and sweetmeats, to destroy Hindoo and Mussulman temples on pretence of making roads, to build churches, to send clergymen into the streets and alleys to preach the Christian religion, to institute English schools and to pay people a monthly stipend for learning the English sciences, while the places of worship of Hindoos and Mussulmans are to this day entirely neglected; with all this, how can the people believe that religion will not be interfered with? The rebellion began with religion, and for it, millions of men have been killed … thousands were hanged rather than abandon their religion.[120]

“THE DEFENCE OF RELIGION WAS THE DOMINANT THEME OF MOST OF THE REBEL PROCLAMATIONS. THE REBELS BELIEVED THAT THE BRITISH WANTED TO CONVERT INDIANS TO CHRISTIANITY.”

polluting. The preservation of religious and caste purity could thus eliminate the possibility of rape.

The aim of the rebels was the destruction of all things British. As William Muir who conducted the enquiry Canning had ordered wrote, 'the object of the mutineers was … not so much to disgrace our name, as to wipe out all traces of Europeans, and of everything connected with foreign rule.' Rape was seen as an instrument of defilement, a mode of domination of women that polluted their blood and body by the most forceful and intimate of interventions. This was not on the rebels' agenda. What drove the rebels was the desire to annihilate the British; this is how the rebels wanted to show and establish their power. The show of power did not distinguish by way of gender or age.

As Russell noted, 'it is clear enough that one of the modes by which the leaders, as if by common instinct, determined to effect their end was the destruction of every white man, woman degrading and horrible experience. It is entirely possible that the issue was enveloped in a silence that the enquiry had failed to penetrate. One district officer noted, 'the investigators themselves are unwilling to inquire minutely or dwell longer on such humiliating subjects.' The absence of rape in 1857, a unique phenomenon, remains an enigma. But as historians we have to depend on the available evidence to reconstruct and understand the past.[119]

The war of religion was justified by a rejection of all things British and all things Christians. The Begum of Awadh retaliated against the Queen's Proclamation thus

> In the Proclamation it is written, that the Christian religion is true, but no other creed will suffer oppression, and that the laws will be observed towards all. What has the administration of justice to do with the truth or falsehood of a religion? That religion is true which acknowledges one God and knows no other. Where there are three Gods in a religion, neither

The rebellion, as this proclamation suggests, completely rejected all the reforms and changes the era of reform under Bentinck and Macaulay had inaugurated. Everything connected with British rule became the rebels' object of hatred. It is not that the rebels only hated and destroyed in the name of religion. They wanted to replace British rule by the world that had been taken away from them. At one level, this world had been taken away from them by the act of annexation. Each act of annexation was seen as an act of deception and treachery. The proclamation that rejected the Queen's Proclamation summed up the reaction to annexation:

> In the Proclamation it is written that all contract and agreements entered into by the Company will be accepted by the Queen. Let the people carefully observe this artifice. The Company had seized on the whole of Hindoostan and if this arrangement be accepted, what is then new in it. The Company professed to treat the chief of

Bhurtpore as a son, and then took his territory. The Chief of Lahore was carried off to London, and it has not fallen to his lot to return, the Nawab Shumshoodeen Khan on one side they hanged, and on the other side, they took off their hats and salaamed to him, the Peshwah they expelled from Poonah Sitara and imprisoned for life in Bithoor, their breach of faith with Sultan Tippoo is well known, the Rajah of Benares they imprisoned in Agra. Under pretence of administering the country of the Chief of Gwalior they introduced English customs, they have left no name or traces of the Chiefs Behar, Orissa and Bengal; they gave the Raes of Farruckabad a small monthly allowance and took his territory. Shajenhanpore, Bareilly, Azimgurh, Jounpore, Gorruckpore, Etawah, Allahabad, Futtehpore etc., our ancient possessions they took from us … they wrote on oath, that they would take no more from us, if then the arrangement made by the Company are to be accepted what is the difference between the former and the present state of things? These are old affairs, but recently, in defiance of treaties and oaths, and notwithstanding that they owed us millions of Rupees, without reason, and on the pretence of the misgovernment and discontent of our people, they took our country and property worth millions of rupees … It is written in the Proclamation that they want no increase of territory but yet they cannot refrain from annexation. If the Queen has assumed the Government why does Her Majesty not restore our country to us when our people wish it?[121]

The demand for restoration was an indicator of the aspirations of the rebel leadership. The revolt almost as soon as it started saw an affiliation with the erstwhile rulers and with rural magnates. These men were accepted as the leaders of the rebellion. In many cases, they were coerced or persuaded to accept the leadership. The three most remarkable instances of this were the three leaders who have assumed iconic status in the annals of the rebellion. They appealed to the old and retired Mughal Emperor, Bahadur Shah, to lead the uprising: his initial reluctance was changed to acceptance by popular pressure from the sepoys who had come to Delhi from Meerut. The Rani of Jhansi was also a reluctant rebel who continued to appeal to the British for terms and for deliverance from the rebels who surrounded her. Nana Sahib too was brought into the folds of the revolt by the insurgents from Kanpur. These leaders may have had their own reasons joining the revolt – they had all suffered in the hands of British rulers – but they waited till the populace around them left them with no choice.

But the question that needs an answer is why the rebels needed the quondam rulers to lead the revolt. This grew out of the rebels' quest for legitimacy. The uprising wanted to affirm itself in the name of a public authority. Having first destroyed all the symbols of British power and having killed the firanghi, the rebels wanted to reconstitute the world. That reconstitution in the India of the mid-nineteenth century and in the context of the rebel consciousness was not possible outside the world of hierarchy. The rebels to establish a legitimacy for themselves appealed to a leader, a king. They harked back to an older political system – the declining Mughal empire of the eighteenth century and the various regional principalities – not because it was idyllic and less oppressive, but because it was familiar. The rebels saw British rule and the imposition of British administration as an alien presence. Social reforms based on the principles of reason, land-revenue administration based on the Ricardian theory of rent, a legal system imported from England, propagation of Christianity and the dispossession of Kings and their successors – these had brought about a major upheaval in North India and had created an enormous amount of disaffection. An entire way of life was going under. A way of life had been dislocated and the people wanted it to be restored.

Hence, the affiliation to the representatives of the previous order: in Delhi to the Mughal Emperor; in Awadh to the boy-king Birjis Qadr, the descendant of the deposed Wajid Ali Shah; in Jhansi to the Rani Lakshmibai; and in Kanpur to the head of the Maratha Confederacy, Nana Sahib, the heir of the Peshwa. The rebels realized that the moment of liberation represented by the destruction of British rule and its symbols could not be sustained for too long, and they accepted that there had to be a return to the old hierarchies.

"THE REBELS WANTED TO ACHIEVE THEIR AIMS BY THE DESTRUCTION OF ALL THINGS BRITISH – EVERY WHITE MAN, WOMAN OR CHILD WHO FELL INTO THEIR HANDS."

A feature of the war of restoration was the leadership the landed magnates – *taluqdars*, *thakurs*, zamindars – provided to the rebellion. Most of the magnates had suffered under British rule. Many had lost their estates in the course of the land revenue settlements the British had carried out and almost all of them had lost their position and status in rural society. The material loss of estates and the 'subjective attachment to traditional status and way of life'[122] made the magnates join the revolt. To this was added in places like Awadh and Jhansi the unpopularity of annexations. One Awadh *taluqdar* told a British officer with tears in his eyes, 'is it justice to turn a deaf ear when the King has sent his very women to plead at the very foot of your throne? Surely not.' The strength of magnate leadership was derived from the support they received from their peasantry. Even peasants who had gained in the land settlements at the expense of the magnates came in to surrender their claims to the land and to declare their allegiance to the magnates. One British officer who was witness to such a show of solidarity in the very early days of the rebellion remembered that 'within one week of the dissolution of Govt.[sic] in the District, the District Officers witnessed Hanwant Singh's courtyard crowded with the very proprietors [the proprietors who had gained from the land settlement] tendering their allegiance to the Talooqdar.'[123]

It is often assumed that the magnates fought within their own territories and seldom widened their political horizon. Thus for the bulk of the rebel forces 'compartmentalism remained the order of the day.'[124] There were too many instances that run counter to this generalization. The classic declaration of aspirations going far beyond his own territory came from Hanwant Singh, the Raja of Kalakankar in southern Awadh, who had lost the bulk of his estate in the Summary Settlement of 1856, and then during the mutiny had provided shelter and protection to the British. He told the British officer whose life he had saved:

> Sahib, your countrymen came into this country and drove out our King. You sent your officers round the districts to examine the titles to the estates. At one blow you took from me lands which from time immemorial had been in my family. I submitted. Suddenly misfortune fell upon you. The people of the land rose against you. You came to me whom you had despoiled I have saved you. But now, I march at the head of my retainers to Lakhnao to drive you from the country.[125]

Other magnates also went out of their territories to fight elsewhere. Mehndi Hussain, the former Raja of Farruckabad, was active in Awadh. So was Khan Bahadur Khan, the rebel leader of Bareilly (Mukherjee: 1984: ch 4). In Bundelkhand, Mardan Singh of Banpur came to Jhansi to organize the resistance there (Roy: 123ff). Feroze Shah fought in Awadh and went on with his troops to join the revolt in central India (Mukherjee: 128). Kunwar Singh marched all the way from Jagdishpur in Bihar to Awadh to give battle.[126] Rana Beni Madho, one of the real heroes of the uprising, fought all over Awadh (Mukherjee: 1984: chs 4 and 5).

It should not also be assumed that the peasants accepted the leadership of the magnates without question. There were instances when the magnates remained loyal to the British but the peasants joined the revolt. In the later stages of the uprising when a British victory had become a certainty, many of the magnates were quick to make peace with the British. There was always the fear of reprisals after the pacification. But the peasants and the sepoys continued to fight in central India and in northern Awadh till disease and death claimed them.

For a little more than a year in 1857-58, prince, magnate and peasant, their many histories and their different aspirations came together to fight the British and redeem their own pasts.

The restorative aspects of the revolt were so preponderant that it is common to label the uprising as retrograde. But this may be too simplistic a notion. The rebels showed a remarkable awareness of the importance of communication in the success of a rebellion. One of the first acts of the rebels in the various stations was to cut off the telegraph wires. In some places, they even cut off postal communications along the Grand Trunk Road, which became a site for a battle to keep the *dak* (post) running along it. The rebels put up placards and posters in front of mosques and issued *ishtahars*. They printed anti-British pamphlets and newspapers and employed the whole range of written indigenous communication – *akhbarats*, *charitas*, *parwanas*, *roznamachas* and so on. They made use of the printing press and lithographed the important proclamation of early August 1857, and even set up their own counter-intelligence and *harkara* system.[127]

The year of the rebellion also saw a flowering of Indian medicine and astrology – forms of knowledge that the British had sought to marginalize by promoting English education and western science. One Pandit Hari Chander incited rebels with his 'knowledge of the stars and the occult sciences.' Native doctors helped to nurse and dress the wounds of the rebels.[128] The revolt was also thus a battleground of ideas.

The influence of the occult was also manifest in the way the rebels perceived their defeat. The appearance of a comet in 1858 gave rise to the feeling among the rebels that defeat and destruction was near and inevitable.[129] Feroze Shah, an important rebel leader believed that the killing of innocent women and children had worked against the insurgents.[130] A group of sepoys confessed,

> Sahib, it has all been the work of fate. After what we had done, we never could fight. No matter whether your troops were black or white, native or European, we could not stand against them; *our salt choked us*.[131]

In a world in which loyalty and honour mattered, a loss of loyalty, an act of *namakharami* (literally going against one's salt; disloyalty) could be seen as the cause of defeat, as the retribution for one's sins. Even in the way the rebels came to terms with their failure, there was a harking back to a traditional world of values and ideas. A familiar world had been taken away by the British and dharma had been threatened. The rebels fought to defend their cherished values and tradition and to enshrine them once again in the world to which they belonged.

UPRISING IN BARRACKPORE

Disarmament of an Indian Regiment at Barrackpore during the revolt in 1857.

> "MANGAL PANDEY'S ATTEMPT AT SUICIDE FAILED: THE BULLET RIPPED APART THE MUSCLES OF HIS CHEST, SHOULDER AND NECK."

Barrackpore in the middle of the 19th century was a sleepy little cantonment town. Its location by the river, and also because it was the country seat of the Governor-General, made it a popular place for visitors from Calcutta. It was the headquarters of the Presidency Division of the army. The first rumblings of discontent within the ranks of the sepoys of the Bengal Army came to Barrackpore and Fort William in Calcutta from Dum Dum. In January 1857, a low caste *khalasi* in Dum Dum asked a Brahmin sepoy for a drink of water from the latter's *lota*. When the sepoy refused saying that his *lota* would be defiled if the *khalasi* touched it, the *khalasi* said, 'You will soon loose your caste, as ere long you will have to bite cartridges covered with the fat of pigs and cows.' The word spread and senior officers received reports from their men about the alarm that was spreading in the sepoy lines about the government's intentions to despoil the caste and religion of the sepoys. On 2 February, in Barrackpore, during the evening parade of the 2nd Native Infantry, the sepoys expressed their mistrust of the new cartridges of the Enfield Rifle. Loyal sepoys reported to their white officers that sepoys were meeting at night to discuss how they would kill the Europeans. The most serious show of defiance came from the 19th Native Infantry which was stationed in Berhampore. Sepoys refused to take the new cartridges and broke open the bell of arms. The British officer had called in the artillery to break the defiance. A full scale mutiny and bloodshed was averted through negotiations. The cartridges of the Enfield Rifle which the sepoys believed were greased with the fat of cows and pigs had clearly created disaffection among the sepoys.

In the bazaars and in the sepoy lines, inaccessible to the British, the rumours of the greased cartridges moved through a 'comradeship response'.

THERE IS NO EVIDENCE THAT MANGAL PANDEY'S ACTIONS HAD ANY IMPACT ON THE REVOLTS THAT TOOK PLACE IN THE GARRISONS OF NORTH INDIA ON OR AFTER 10 MAY.

The peace in Barrackpore was broken on 29 April 1857. It was a Sunday afternoon when a sepoy of the 34th Native Infantry named Mangal Pandey was found in the parade ground in a dhoti and his regimental jacket with a loaded musket shouting at his fellow sepoys to join him in defending their caste and religion. He fired at a British sergeant, Hewson, who went to disarm him but missed. He then fired at Lieutenant Baugh and brought down his horse. When Baugh charged at him, Mangal Pandey slashed at him with his sword. Baugh's life was saved by a sepoy called Sheikh Pultoo who restrained Mangal Pandey. More than 400 sepoys were onlookers to this incident and some of them even hit Baugh from behind with their rifle butts. The regimental commander Colonel Wheeler arrived on the scene and ordered the regimental *jemadar* to arrest Mangal Pandey. The *jemadar* refused. By this time General Hearsey, the officer commanding Barrackpore, arrived on the scene and rode up to Mangal Pandey who turned his musket upon himself and pulled the trigger with his foot. He only succeeded in injuring himself and in setting his jacket on fire. He was arrested and tried. In his trial, Mangal Pandey, despite repeated requests, refused to speak. He admitted that he had lately been taking *bhang* and had not been aware of what he was doing on that Sunday. His previous conduct was reported to be good. He was hanged on 7 April in the presence of all the troops in Barrackpore. Conventionally, Mangal Pandey's show of defiance has been seen as the beginning of the uprising of 1857. It is also said that it was his name that made the British call mutinous sepoys by the epithet Pandy. Both claims might be slightly exaggerated. There is no evidence that Mangal Pandey's actions had any impact on the mutinies that took place in the garrisons of North India on and after 10 May. There are no contemporary legends and folk songs about Mangal Pandey. In fact, except his name, age, length of service and his regiment nothing else is known about him. His actions were obviously situated in an atmosphere of fear and discontent that prevailed in the sepoy lines in Barrackpore and elsewhere, but Mangal Pandey was alone in his defiance. The move from individual defiance to collective rebellion was to take place in Meerut on 10 May and in other cantonments after the fall of Delhi on 11-12 May. The name epithet Pandy was probably derived from the fact that most of the sepoys of the Bengal Army were Brahmins from Awadh, and many of them bore the surname Pandey. The term Pandy used pejoratively by British soldiers and officers to describe all rebels was probably not derived from the surname of just one sepoy.

Throughout the summer of 1857 when mutiny after mutiny occurred in the stations of North India, Barrackpore remained quiet as did Calcutta and most other places in the region. The uprising of 1857 was a North Indian affair. It might thus be simplistic to see Mangal Pandey as the first rebel and Barrackpore as the first site of the rebellion.

A statue of Mangal Pandey unveiled by the Indian Army at Barrackpore in the latter part of the twentieth century.

UPRISING IN MEERUT

The march of sepoys from Meerut to Delhi led to the spread of revolt in the Gangetic plain.

“THE REVOLT BROKE AFTER 5 IN THE EVENING AS THE BRITISH COMMUNITY WAS GETTING READY TO ATTEND THE SERVICE.”

On 23 April 1857 Colonel Carmichael Smyth who commanded the 3rd Native Cavalry at Meerut ordered a parade of ninety sepoys to be held next morning. The purpose of the parade was to show the men a method of loading their carbines without biting the cartridges. During the parade, all but five refused to take the cartridges. Carmichael Smyth's exhortations were in vain. A court of enquiry was ordered and the sepoys were tried by a Native Court Martial. The sepoys were sentenced to ten years of rigorous imprisonment. On the morning of 9 May with the whole brigade watching, the convicted men were stripped off their uniform and had fetters put on their hands and feet. The sepoys who watched the proceedings were clearly unhappy in the manner their comrades were being treated. Many observers felt that if British troops had not been present an outbreak could easily have occurred. The convicted men, once they realized what they were losing, broke down completely. But the morning passed without incident. At night, loyal sepoys informed some British officers that a mutiny would take place the next day. But the officers ignored such warnings as idle gossip. Sunday, 10 May 1857, began quietly in Meerut. The mutiny broke after 5 in the evening as the British community was getting ready to attend the evening service. Very significantly, the first thing that sowars of the 3rd cavalry did was to rush to the old prison and free their comrades. The sepoys of the 20th Native Infantry entered the parade ground and broke into the bell of arms. The mutiny in Meerut had begun. No one could predict then the direction it would take and the dimensions it would acquire.

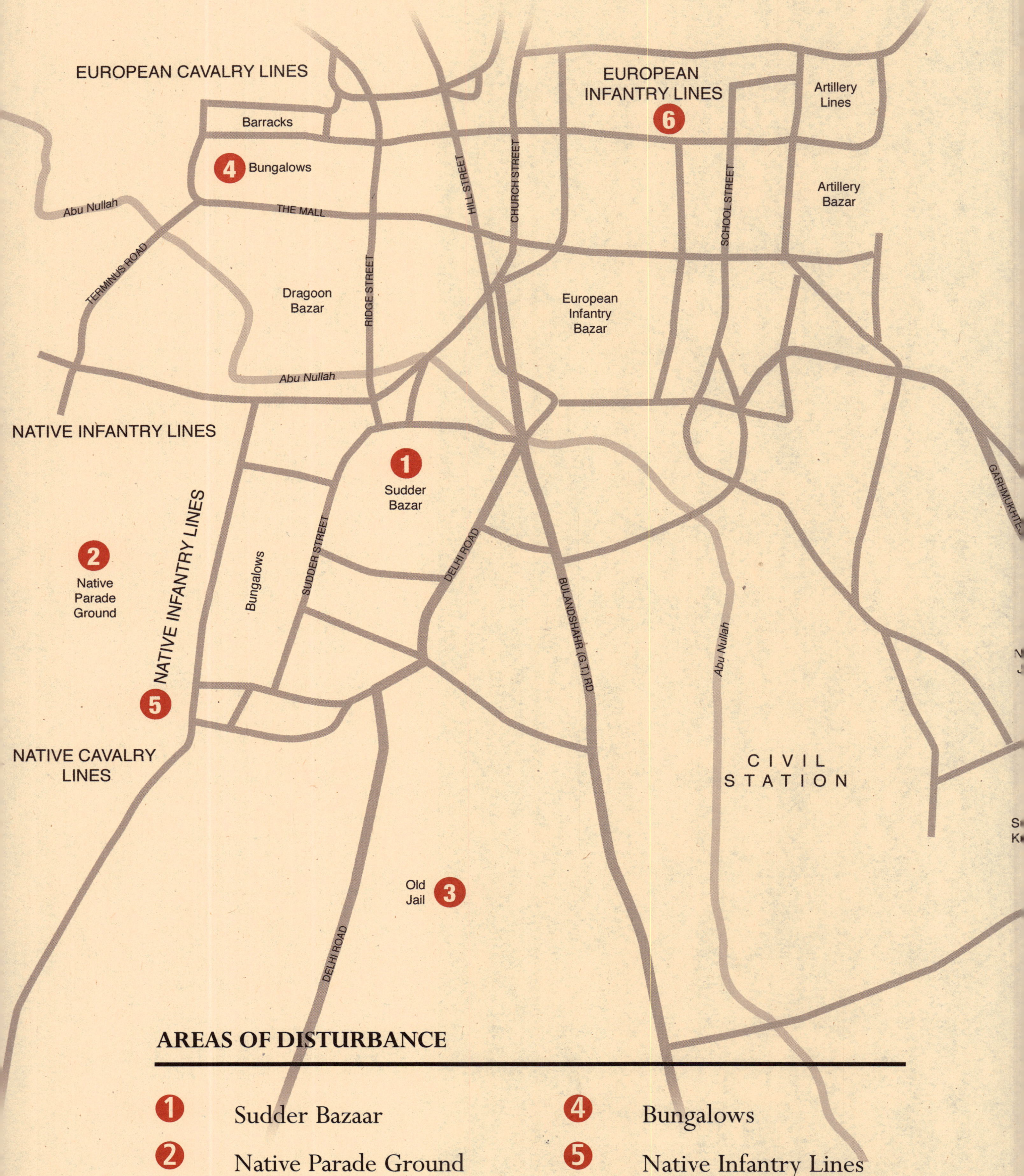

AREAS OF DISTURBANCE

1	Sudder Bazaar	4	Bungalows
2	Native Parade Ground	5	Native Infantry Lines
3	Old Jail	6	European Infantry Lines

> **THE REVOLT IN MEERUT SET THE PATTERN FOR THE SUBSEQUENT REVOLTS IN THE CANTONMENTS THAT DOTTED NORTH INDIA.**

The direction that the mutiny would take became apparent as night fell and a group of sepoys rode off towards Delhi. Arriving there early in the morning of 11 May, the sepoys appealed to the Mughal Emperor, Bahadur Shah, old and decrepit though he was, to accept the leadership of the rebellion. It had already become evident as events had unfolded in Meerut that the mutiny was acquiring the dimensions of a general uprising. In Meerut, the sepoys had first broken open the jail and had taken over the bell of arms. After that they had proceeded to destroy and burn all government property – the court, the record room, the bungalows in which the white people lived. Simultaneously, there was the killing of all Europeans. Women and children were not spared and only a fortunate few escaped the wrath of the rebels. The anger of the rebels was also directed at those who were seen to be friends of the British, like the Bengalis. In Meerut, the wine shop owned by Kailash Chandra Ghosh was attacked. The people of the town and from the surrounding villages joined the sepoys in the destruction and the killing. According to the official narrative of events for Meerut, 'the residents of the wretched hamlets poured out to share in what they evidently knew was going to happen.' There was in fact a coming together of the sepoy elements and the common people. The sepoys often shed their uniform as they went about killing and destroying. This meant that sepoys in the moment of mutiny cast off the markers with which an alien power had sought to regiment them and thus set them apart from the peasantry from which the sepoys had been recruited. Of course, the one marker they would not jettison was their arms. The 'peasant in uniform' – as the sepoy was – disowned his uniform only to become the peasant with arms. In eschewing the regimental discipline that the British officers had drilled into them, they reclaimed their peasant character. They merged with the ordinary people. This merger is significant since it signals the extension of the mutinies to a general uprising.

The mutiny in Meerut set the pattern for the subsequent mutinies in the cantonments that dotted North India. In almost all these places, the sepoys began the mutiny by taking over the bell of arms and destroying government property and bungalows in which the British lived. The jail, the court and the record room were common targets of attack. Another common feature was the killing of the white man or the *firanghi*, as he was commonly referred to. Again in most places, the killing was indiscriminate of gender and age. In every station, once the sepoys had mutinied they were joined in the killing and the destruction by the common people. The villagers and the townfolk joined the sepoys everywhere. The mutinies almost as soon as they occurred became a general uprising with the merging of the sepoys with the common people. There is another common aspect to be noted. Some of the sepoys of Meerut went off to Delhi to appeal to Bahadur Shah to be the leader. In places like Lucknow and Kanpur too the rebels turned to the local leaders – the ruling dynasty of Awadh in Lucknow, and the Nana Sahib in Kanpur – for leadership.

UPRISING IN DELHI

Ruins of the Bank House at Delhi, property of Dyce Sombre's family, also known as Begum Samroo's Mahal. The mahal now houses the famous wholesale market of electrical goods, Bhagirath Palace.

"THE KING RESIGNED HIMSELF TO THE INEVITABLE AND ACCEPTED THE LEADERSHIP OF THE REVOLT."

11 May 1857 was the sixteenth day of the holy month of Ramadan. The old Mughal Emperor, Bahadur Shah had just finished his morning prayers when around 7 a.m. he noticed smoke arising from the bridge of boats across the Jamuna. His enquiries revealed that some sepoys had arrived from Meerut. They had killed the toll collector and set fire to his office. Very soon the sepoys were clamouring outside the Lal Qila demanding to see the Emperor. They refused to go away and some of them slipped into the city before all the gates could be shut. Inside the city, as the word spread that the sepoys had killed the Europeans in Meerut, people began to gather around and the atmosphere became tense. The sepoys first moved into the palace where the guards offered them no resistance. Inside the palace, they murdered Simon Fraser, the Commissioner, J.R. Hutchinson, the Collector and Captain Douglas who commanded the palace guards. The chaplain and his family met the same fate. The soldiers entered the king's private chambers and demanded that the king assume leadership of the rebellion they had started. Bahadur Shah was utterly helpless: he was surrounded by rebels who had violated the sanctity of the palace, and who were turning increasingly violent. He resigned himself to the inevitable and accepted the leadership of the revolt. This boosted the morale of the rebels but sealed Bahadur Shah's fate.

While within the palace, the sepoys forced the hand of Emperor, the city was engulfed in violence. Every single Christian, European and Indian, the rebels could lay their hands on were killed. A handful had miraculous escapes. The bank was looted, its manager and his family murdered. The office of the local newspaper was attacked and burnt. Those who were taken prisoner were later killed. The British were forced to abandon the city and evacuate the cantonment. But the magazine was not left unprotected even though it had only nine Britons to protect it. It was decided to blow up the magazine as the crowd outside it grew more menacing. The crowd demanded that the nine surrender and began to fix ladders to assault the place. Lieutenant Willoughby who was in charge gave a signal, agreed upon from before, and the train was lit. A tremendous explosion announced that the magazine was gone, but the explosion took with it three of the nine Britons. For the next few weeks, there were no battles in Delhi, the rebels were left alone by the British. But the sepoys did not leave the Emperor alone. They wanted pay and provisions. Bahadur Shah was in no position to provide these. On 12 May, he summoned some Muslim nobles to advise him. A governor was appointed and Mirza Mughal was made Commander-in-Chief. Attempts were made to restore order in the city and the Emperor appealed to shopkeepers and traders to resume their business. But it proved impossible to control the sepoys who continued with their loot and plunder. There was the awareness that the British counter-attack to recapture the city would not be long in coming.

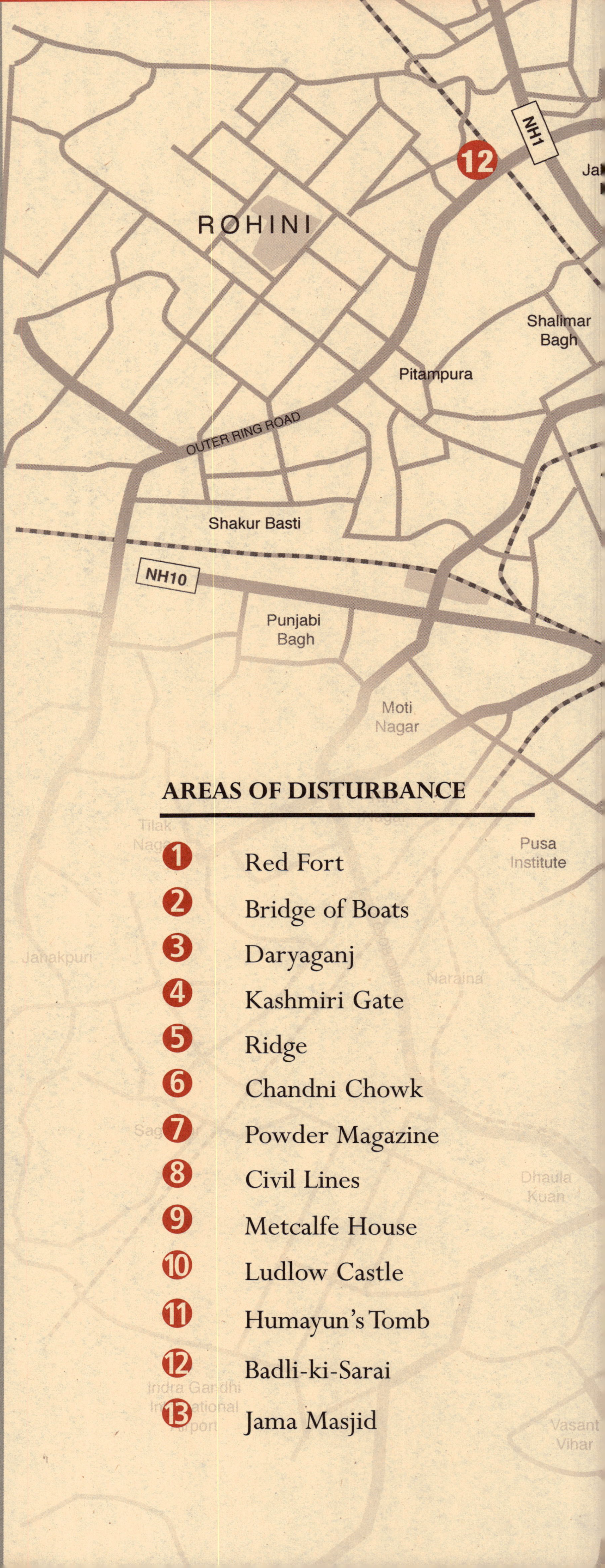

DATELINE 1857
Revolt Against the Raj
Yamuna
OUTER RING ROAD
Model Town
G.T. ROAD
Kamla Nagar
9
5
8
Ridge
10
SHAHDARA
NH24
Gandhi Nagar
Vishwas Nagar
4
7
1
Yamuna
Sadar Bazar
6
13
2
Anand Vihar
3
Laxmi Nagar
Connaught Place
Shakarpur
IP Extension
NH24 BYPASS
Patparganj
India Gate
Mayur Vihar Phase I
11
Lodi Colony
NOIDA
Yamuna
Sarojini Nagar
RING ROAD
Lajpat Nagar
NH2
AIIMS
East of Kailash
Okhla
GK I

Ludlow Castle: The new Residency office built by Dr Ludlow. It stood outside the city walls in the Civil Lines and on 7 September 1857, the first battery was established by the British forces near this residence. It had to be taken from the rebels during the battle for Delhi.

The British attack came on 8 June when a battle was fought in Badli-ki-Serai, five miles from Delhi, led by General Henry Barnard. The rebels were roundly defeated with the loss of twenty-six guns. The British lost four officers and several were wounded. The victorious army pushed forward and occupied the Ridge, which the rebels failed to defend. The British were thus back in the cantonment that they had vacated on 11 May. Barnard decided not to attack the city immediately but he occupied a few crucial posts and placed picquets there. Perhaps the most important of these were Hindu Rao's house near Sabzi Mandi, and the Flagstaff Tower, a round, two-storeyed building made of brick which served as an excellent observation post. The rebels kept attacking the British posts and they certainly had the greater artillery power. On 19 June, the rebels threatened the rear of the British forces but failed to cut off the communication with Punjab. On the centenary of Plassey (23 June), the rebels, believing in the prophecy that the Company's rule would come to an end on that day, fought desperately but without too much success. The rebel army in Delhi received reinforcements from Bareilly on 1 and 2 July. Bakht Khan, the Commander of the Bareilly troops, waited on the Emperor on 2 July and offered him his services. He was appointed Commander-in-Chief over Mirza Mughal who was made Adjutant-General. On 14 July, the rebels attacked Hindu Rao's house and the picquets in Sabzi Mandi. The rebel army was covered by heavy artillery fire from the city walls. The battle lasted the whole day and was inconclusive.

Hindu Rao's House: The house of Hindu Rao from the state of Gwalior was formely the residence of Mr William Fraser, commissioner of Delhi. In 1857, this house formed the headquarters of the centre of the British position. The building was the special mark of the sepoy's artillery and was cause of wonder to all at the end of the siege as to how the walls still stood. This photograph was taken around September 1857, by Bourne and Shepherd.

Jama Masjid, the mosque where Bahadur Shah Zafar used to offer namaz every Friday was occupied by the British Army and was locked against worshippers till 1862. Fortunately it escaped demolition, a measure of retribution against the Muslims of Delhi that was suggested in 1857. This photograph was taken by Felice Beato in 1858.

INSET: Colour portrait of Bahadur Shah Zafar made for Theophilus John Metcalfe in 1844.

Bones of the sepoys killed by the British near Delhi during the Indian rebellion of 1857. Fierce battles were fought at Badli-ki-sarai, Mori Bastion, Kashmiri Bastion and near Najafgarh village.

Metcalfe House: Built by Thomas Metcalfe, Resident at Delhi, when he decided to make India his home. According to his son, Charles Theophilus Metcalfe, Metcalfe senior stripped his family treasures in England, little apprehending the fate in store, all destroyed in one morning by the villagers of Chandrowli. All the trees in the huge garden were cut and besides the injury caused by fire; the house was considerably knocked about by shot and shell during the siege of 1857. The building was later restored and now houses the Defence Research Development Office (DRDO) of the Indian Government.

INSET: John Theophilus Metcalfe.

On 1 August came Id. There was the fear that there would be an outbreak of hostility between Hindus and Muslims in Delhi. This apprehension grew from the fact that a large number of people declaring themselves to be *jihadis* had arrived in Delhi. The *jihadis* were not trained soldiers but they were fearless in facing death. The Emperor appealed for unity and after the morning prayers, the rebels opened a vigorous attack on British positions. The battle raged through the afternoon into the night and continued till noon the next day. The rebels faced a heavy fire but they continued to fight. Despite their courage, the British could not be dislodged. Rebel morale struck a new low when their magazine was exploded on 7 August. On the same day, John Nicholson rode into the British camp in advance of his column which arrived seven days later. The column had 2,000 infantry, six guns and some cavalry.

Tree in Palace (Lal Quila) where forty-nine Christians were murdered on 15 May 1857. Confined in a room of the king's kitchen, 40 ft long and 12 ft broad, these Christians were killed by the king's servants.

FACING PAGE: Native officers of Hodson's Horse, a cavalry regiment which originated as part of the British Indian Army. Raised by Brevet Major William Stephen Raikes Hodson, during the uprising in India in 1857, the regiment still exists in the Indian Army as the 4th Horse Regiment.

For the recovery of Delhi, the British had arranged for a siege train to arrive to help Nicholson. When the rebels learnt of this, they marched out on 24 August with eighteen guns to intercept it. Nicholson followed the next day to stop the rebel army. The two armies met near Najafgarh and the rebel army was defeated after a hard fought encounter. Nicholson returned to the Ridge and the siege train with thirty pieces of heavy ordnance and plenty of ammunition arrived on 3 September. The stage was now set for the battle for Delhi. The assault began on the morning of 11 September. Nicholson divided his assaulting force into four columns. One under his own command to take the Kashmir Bastion; the second led by Brigadier Jones to take the Water Bastion; the third commanded by Colonel Campbell was to blow up the Kashmir Gate; and the fourth under Major Reid was to enter the city through the Lahore Gate. All four columns faced stiff resistance. Major Reid's force had to retreat after suffering heavy casualties from artillery fire from the Lahore Gate. Nicholson's force was stopped at the Kabul Gate where Nicholson himself fell. Jones's column had also to fall back. It was only the third column under Campbell that succeeded: it blew up the Kashmir Gate and, despite casualties, marched into the city up to the Jama Masjid. Thus at the end of the day, the British had a foothold in the city and parts of the city wall had been breached. The losses were severe: 1,104 men and 66 officers were killed or wounded. From the 16 to 19 September the British advanced their position, and on the 20th the palace and the adjoining fort of Selimgarh was entered. No one found in the palace was spared his life. The occupation of Delhi was complete bar the last tragic act.

Brigadier John Nicholson's grave: John Nicholson was a key figure in the British recapture of Delhi, and notorious for his ruthless treatment of rebels. He died on 23 September 1857 during the assault on Delhi and was buried in Nicholson's cemetery near Kashmiri Gate. Inscribed on his grave stone is 'The grave of Brigadier John Nicholson who led the assault of Delhi but fell in the hour of victory, mortally wounded and died 23rd September 1857 aged 35.'

ABOVE: Lt CH Mecham (centre) and Lt Surgeon Anderson (seated right) of the British Hodson's Horse cavalry regiment in India during the mutiny.
BELOW: Warriors of the Indian Hindu Rajput caste, 1857.

ABOVE: Humayun's Tomb: In September 1857 Delhi fell, and Bahadur Shah Zafar withdrew with his sons and grandson to Humayun's Tomb. But his location was betrayed to Captain Hodson, the leader of the British forces in Delhi. He was arrested on 20 September 1857, while his sons were shot.
BELOW: Diwan-i-khas at the King's Palace, the Red Fort was used and misused by the British after 1857. In 1858 this hall of special audience was also used as the trial court of Bahadur Shah Zafar and later used by the British to host parties and dinners.

As it became clear that Delhi would fall to the British, Bahadur Shah had decided on his own future. Before dawn on 17 September, he slipped out of the Lal Qila through the water gate with a few attendants and a selection of his ancestral treasures. At dawn he took a boat down the Jamuna to the Purana Qila from where he made his way to the Sufi shrine of Nizamuddin. He deposited the treasures at the shrine, prayed and had a simple breakfast. He proceeded to his summer palace in Mehrauli but returned when he was informed that Gujars were robbing people along that road. He made his way to the tomb of Humayun, the first great monument the Mughals had built in India. On 21 September, William Hodson arrived at the tomb with a small force and took Bahadur Shah prisoner. He escorted him back to Lal Qila. The last Mughal Emperor came back to his ancestral dwellings as a prisoner. The next day Hodson returned to arrest the three princes. On the way back, a few miles before the walls of Delhi, Hodson ordered the three princes to get out of the cart and to strip naked. He then shot them in cold blood. He pocketed whatever jewels they had and left the bodies in front of the *kotwali*. What followed was a general massacre of the populace of Delhi. The cycle of vengeance was complete.

Bahadur Shah Zafar and his sons near Humayun's Tomb, being arrested by Captain Hodson. Though the king was arrested, he was guaranteed life on General Wilson's – Commander of the Delhi Field Force – order.

This Felice Beato photograph is of the house in which Bahadur Shah Zafar was confined in the palace during his trial. The king was brought to trial under Act XIV of 1857 before a special Commission, which lasted twenty-one days. This special act passed on 6 June 1857, made a provision for punishment of persons convicted exciting revolt or sedition in the army. The offender was also liable to the punishment of death and forfeiture of all his property.

John Lawrence was Viceroy of India from 1863-69. During the revolt, he was Chief Commissoner of Punjab and his support to the British troops fighting to recapture Delhi was critical to their success.

British troops near the mosque at Khynabee Gate, Delhi, during the uprising against the British.

In the campaign to recapture Delhi, the British destroyed and damaged many buildings. Mosques like Fatehpuri as well as the Jama Masjid were taken over by the British troops. Though Jama Masjid was just closed for worship, some other mosques were damaged brutally and used by the British soldiers as sites for liquor parties. Constructed by Qudsia Begum, the chief queen of Mughal Emperor Muhammed Shah, the mosque in this photograph of the Qudsia Bagh was the private mosque of the emperor and his wife. This mosque too was badly damaged during the 1857 uprising.

ABOVE: Kashmiri Gate: A site of fierce fighting.
BELOW: Flagstaff Tower: The tower served as a hiding place for British women and children before they were moved to Karnal. Later the rebels made their last stand against the British at this tower before retreating into the old city to face eventual defeat.

ABOVE: A Felice Beato photograph of rebels at gallows: It was common to hang 'rebels' publicly to serve as a warning to avoid future betrayals.
BELOW: Officers present at the siege of Delhi.

UPRISING IN LUCKNOW

View of an Indian rebel being executed by canon.

"IN LUCKNOW AS SOON AS THE SEPOYS HAD RISEN, THE COMMON PEOPLE OF THE CITY OPENLY EXPRESSED THEIR HOSTILITY TO THE BRITISH."

As the news of the fall of Delhi travelled down the Ganges valley, garrison after garrison went up in mutiny. The news of the mutinies reached Lucknow at the end of May. For some time before that signs of discontent had been visible in the city. Many religious leaders came to the capital of Awadh and spoke of the intentions of the government to despoil the caste and religion of Indians. In Lucknow, another important source of grievance was the annexation of Awadh and the treatment that had been meted out to Wajid Ali Shah by the British. Wajid Ali Shah, contrary to British views, had been a popular figure in Awadh and his exile from his beloved Lucknow cast a permanent shadow on the people and their emotions. Proclamations and prophecies about the impending end of British rule were common in the city just before the mutiny broke on the evening of 30 May. The mutiny began with the firing of the evening gun and violence engulfed the British and all that symbolized their rule. One significant feature of the mutiny in Lucknow was that as soon as the sepoys had risen, the common people of the city also openly displayed their hostility to British rule. Just as the fall of Delhi was followed by mutinies in the stations of the Gangetic plain, the mutiny in Lucknow was the signal for mutinies to take place in the various districts of Awadh. Very soon British authority had disappeared in the districts of Awadh and the only place where British authority was visible was in the Residency in Lucknow.

By the end of June rebels from all the districts of Awadh had started moving into Lucknow. They were apparently in communication with the Nana Sahib in Kanpur. As soon as the news of the fall of the entrenchment in Kanpur reached Lucknow, the onslaught on the Residency began. The rebels had been joined by some of the *taluqdars* and members of the Nawabi bureaucracy. One of the first to join had been the Nawab of Mahumudabad. One estimate said that the rebel army was about 7,000 and had many guns. The first encounter with the British took place at Chinhat where the British were defeated.

AREAS OF DISTURBANCE

1. British Residency
2. Bara Imambara
3. Chhota Imambara
4. Kaiser Bagh Palace
5. Bridge of Boats
6. Chattar Manzil
7. Machchi Bhawan
8. Rumi Darwaza
9. Hazratganj
10. Cantonment
11. Civil Lines
12. La Martiniere
13. Alambagh

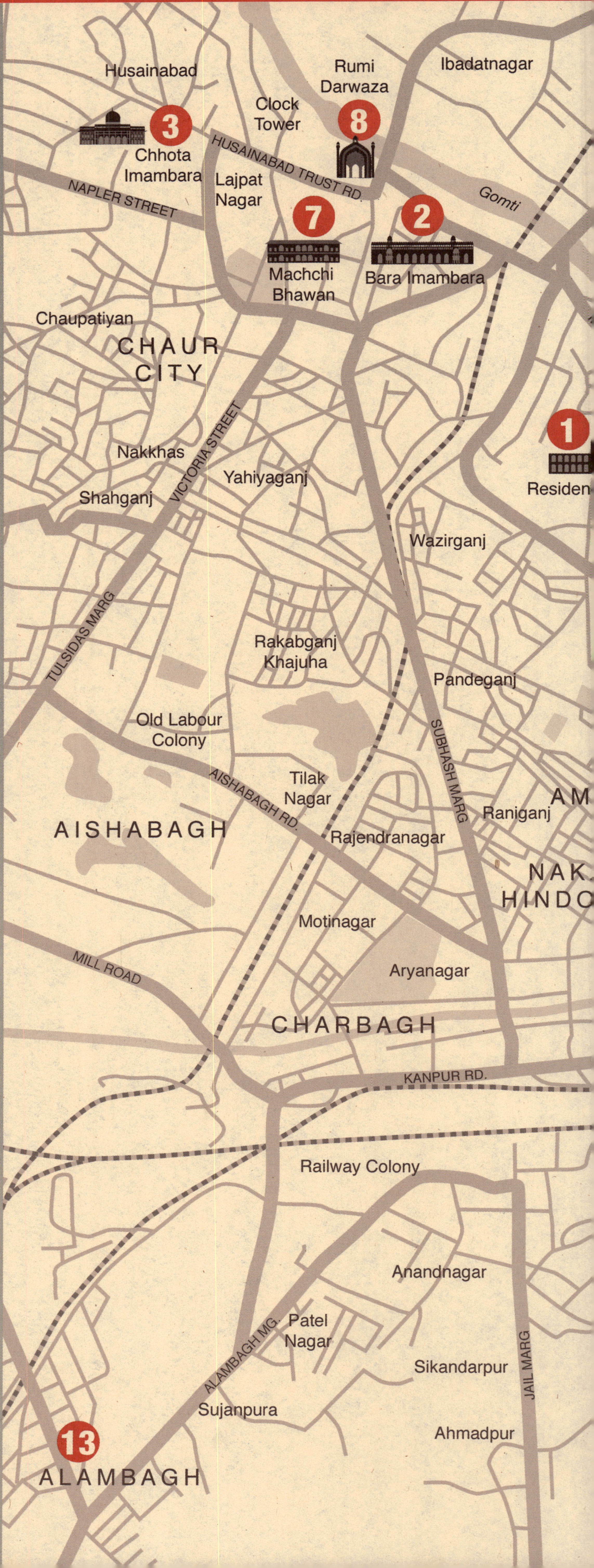

NIRALA NAGAR
MAHANAGAR COLONY
DALIGANJ
ACHARYA NARENDRADEV MARG
FAIZABAD RD. (NH 28)
Railway Colony
Paper Mill Colony
Balmikinagar
Gomti
6
Chattar Manzil
11
CIVIL LINES
Butler Colony
Lal Baradari
4
Kaisarbagh
9
Hazratganj
Lalbagh
VIDHAN SABHA MG.
Banarsi Bagh
12
La Martiniere
5
Bridge of Boats
GANESH GANJ
Gautampalli
MOTILAL NEHRU MG.
CANTONMENT RD.
MAHATMA GANDHI MG.
VIKRAMADITYA MARG
The Mall Avenue
Gulistan Colony
Sadr Bazar
Play Ground
Polo Ground
10
CANTONMENT
CARIAPPA RD.
RAE BARELI RD.

Raja Man Singh of Faizabad: During the uprising, Man Singh, one of the most prominent *taluqdars* of Awadh, saved the lives of a very large number of European refugees, and though at first for some time he took part with the rebels, he subsequently strenuously assisted the government in the suppression of the revolt and the restoration of order.

Ruins of the Residency showing the room where Sir Henry Lawrence was killed. Formely occupied by Lawrence, Chief Commissioner of Awadh at the outbreak of the revolt, the Residency became the last defended place for the British. The building was crammed with soldiers and civilians fighting for their lives. The posed figure on the far right stands in front of the room where Lawrence was killed. The Residency was reopened for the public exactly 100 years after in 1957 and is maintained in the same condition as it was in 1857.

The siege of the Lucknow Residency began as soon as the British forces suffered their first defeat at the battle of Chinhat on 30 June 1857. Immediately, after this setback, Henry Lawrence, the Chief Commissioner of Awadh, retreated with his entire force and dependents into the 37 acre compound of the Residency, which was surrounded on all sides by rebels who carried out a constant shelling of the place. The situation was so desperate that Henry Lawrence thought they could hold out for merely fifteen or twenty days.

In early July, shortly after dawn one day Henry Lawrence came back to his room in the Residency after having done his round of all the posts. The previous day a howitzer shell had burst in his room but he had escaped unhurt. His staff had requested him to move to a room that was less exposed. Henry Lawrence had agreed to do it the next day; he did not believe that there was so good a marksman as to shell the same place twice. But this is exactly what happened. While he was dictating a memorandum, a second shell burst in the room and seriously injured Henry Lawrence. The doctor gave him forty hours to live. He died on 4 July. He was given a quiet burial and for the next few days his death was kept a secret.

Once Kanpur had been recaptured from the rebels in July 1857, British forces moved towards Lucknow to relieve the Residency inside which Britons were in a terrible plight. This force was under the command of Major General Henry Havelock and was joined by Sir James Outram as a volunteer. The force, as it moved towards Lucknow, encountered very heavy resistance especially in the villages of Unao. It became clear from the nature of this resistance that what the British were facing was not a mere military mutiny, but a resistance that had a popular base among the peasants of Awadh. Havelock entered the Residency in September 1857, but was unable to provide any relief to it since the British forces remained surrounded on all sides and faced an acute shortage of supplies. Attempts to procure supplies from the city and from the neighbourhood failed, confirming the impression that resistance to the British was popular. Thus what is known as the First Relief of Lucknow was no relief at all. In fact, as has rightly been pointed out, the siege of the Residency became a blockade.

The mine in the Chattar Manzil exploded by the army at the first attack of General Havelock .

Sir Colin Campbell (right), 1st Baron Clyde. A general of tried experience, Colin Campbell was called with a command from London. After spending two months in Calcutta organizing his resources, he started for the front on 27 October 1857, and on 17 November 1858 relieved Lucknow for the second time. Campbell is seen here with William Mansfield, 1st Baron Sandhurst, Governor of Bombay.

Major General Sir James Outram, the first chief commissioner of Awadh, after its annexation, was appointed in 1857 to command the two divisions of the Bengal Army occupying the country from Calcutta to Kanpur.

One of the first things that Campbell did on entering Lucknow was to evacuate the British from the city. But this act only encouraged the rebels. It was proclaimed in the city that the Europeans had abandoned the place and crowds of people flocked to the capital from the districts to take part in the struggle. By January, Lucknow was swarming with fighting men. After the evacuation of Lucknow, Campbell withdrew to Lucknow leaving Outram with 4,000 men to control Alambagh. The position of the latter force was vulnerable in the extreme. No supplies were forthcoming and the entire populace was hostile. Outram's garrison was reduced to inactivity. Anti-British feelings ran high and popular opinion believed that the British were on the losing side.

First attack of Sir Colin Campbell in November 1857 – the Mess House of 32nd Regiment. According to Francis Cornwallis Maude, a British officer who observed the attack on the Mess House, Campbell 'treated this building to a bombardment of 10 hours after it had been abandoned by its defenders'. The white marks in the photograph are the repairs later made by the rebels.

First attack of Sir Colin Campbell, the tomb of Saadut Ali Khan in Kaiser Bagh Palace. Hugely destroyed by the attack, the tomb now stands devoid of its elaborate enclosures and gates.

First attack of Sir Colin Campbell: Originally named 'Constantia', La Martiniere was designed by Major General Claude Martin, who arrived in India from France in 1751. In 1857 British troops were also stationed in this beautiful school as per the orders of the Chief Commissioner, Henry Lawrence. After the fierce fighting nothing remained but the bullet and shot ridden walls. Doors and windows had vanished, marble pavements dug up, the library destroyed, the ornamented ceilings and interiors riddled with musket ball and ironwork removed. It is the only school in the world to have been awarded Battle Honours for the part the staff and pupils played in the Defence of the Residency at Lucknow.

First attack of Sir Colin Campbell – the interiors of the Sikandarabagh after the massacre of two thousand rebels by the 93rd Highlanders and 4th Punjab Regiment, November 1857. According to popular legend, Felice Beato especially had the bones and skulls dug out for this photograph.

Breach in the wall and gateway of Sikandara Bagh after the first attack of Sir Colin Campbell. This view shows the formal exterior wall of the Sikandara Bagh, a small wall garden on the outskirts of the city. The figure standing in profile on the right of the building marks the position of the breach which was opened on 16 November 1857, allowing the British to gain access to the garden.

Second attack of Sir Colin Campbell in March 1858, the small Imambara Magazine.

Raja Dirgbijay Singh of Balrampur. The most steadfast ally of the British in Awadh, the raja joined the British forces under the command of Sir Hope Grant. He was also instrumental in procuring supplies and obtaining accurate information about the movements of the rebels.

Son of Raja of Gonda, 1858. On the outbreak of revolt, the raja of Gonda, after honourably escorting the government treasure to Faizabad, joined the rebels. His estates were confiscated and conferred as rewards upon the maharajas of Balrampur and Ayodhya, who had remained loyal to the British.

ABOVE: Second attack of Sir Colin Campbell: The Begum Kothi, Lucknow.
BELOW: Second attack of Sir Colin Campbell: Exterior of Asaf-ud-Daula's tomb.

ABOVE: Indian Mutiny group at Alambagh.
BELOW: Indian Mutiny group at Lucknow.

Relief of Lucknow: Triumphant meeting of Sir Henry Havelock, Sir James Outram and Sir Colin Campbell: In October 1857, word came that a force was on the way to rescue soldiers and civilians confined to the Residency. The force was led by Sir Colin Campbell, a Crimean war veteran. An Irish post office worker at the Residency, Henry Kavanagh came forward and volunteered to slip out of the Residency, make contact with the relief column and guide it back through the city. Wearing Indian clothes and his face blackened with oil, he made his way past sepoy checkpoints, swam the Gomti and found a British picket. Eight days later he returned and led Havelock and Outram through the streets to a meeting with their rescuer, Sir Colin Campbell.

The bridge of boats over the Gomti in Lucknow crossed by Sir James Outram at the capture of Lucknow, 1858. This bridge of boats built by the British engineers in front of the La Martiniere helped Sir James Outram lead his troops through the outskirts of the city for a strategic attack on the rebels.

The much-awaited Relief of Lucknow came in the middle of November when Colin Campbell marched into the city with his troops. But before this, in the period between Havelock's entry into Lucknow and Campbell's, the city was the scene of very heavy fighting. Both the rebels and the British realized the symbolic power of controlling the capital of Awadh. Outram wrote, 'I regard the reestablishment of our government as an impossibility, so long as the capital, which is looked upon by every native as the seat of government is in the hands of the rebels.' The importance of Lucknow in the eyes of the rebels is evident from the concentration of their forces in the city. Around October 1857, twelve infantry and three cavalry regiments were reported to be fighting in the city. The Bailee Guard was surrounded on all sides. Fighting was particularly heavy on 16, 17 and 18 November when Campbell's relief force finally entered Lucknow. Streets were blocked up with dead bodies.

As the British forces conquered area after area in North India and closed in on Awadh, preparations mounted on the rebel side to defend Lucknow. Men and levies from all over were coming into the city to help in the defence. The rebels knew it was a matter of time before Colin Campbell was back with his force to reconquer Lucknow and Awadh. There was also a general recognition among the rebels that the tide had turned against them. They had failed to take the Residency, stop the relief forces first under Havelock and Outram and then under Campbell, and subsequently to defeat Outram at Alambagh. Begum Hazrat Mahal herself noted this when she wrote, 'The whole army is in Lucknow, but it is without courage. Why does it not attack the Alambagh? Is it waiting for the English to be reinforced, and Lucknow to be surrounded?'

Rumi Darwaza and the Imambara

Campbell began his movement towards Lucknow at the end of February, by the end of March the place was said to be free of the rebels. Campbell met strong resistance but it was nowhere near what one would expect from the number of fighting men in the city. The rebels maintained a constant cannonading of the British; most of the palaces had to be breached and Outram's progress from Alambagh into the city was halted again and again by the rebels. The British troops were fired upon from houses in the narrow lanes. The most severe resistance came from within the Begum's palace. The British captured Lucknow but some thousands of rebels escaped from the city into the countryside.

Second attack of Sir Colin Campbell: Kaiser Bagh Palace.

The fall of Lucknow was followed by scenes of loot and plunder. According to *The Times*, the loot amounted to a million and quarter sterling. The correspondent of *The Times*, William Howard Russell left the following description of the sack of Kaiserbagh: 'The scene of plunder was indescribable. The soldiers had broken up several of the store rooms, and pitched the contents into the court, which was lumbered with cases, with embroidered clothes, gold and silver brocade, silver vessels, arms, banners, drums, shawls, scarves, musical instruments, mirrors, pictures, books, accounts, medicine bottles, gorgeous standards, shields, spears, and a heap of things ... Through these moved the men, wild with excitement, ``drunk with plunder". I had often heard the phrase, but never saw the thing itself before. They smashed to pieces the fowling-pieces and pistols to get at the gold mountings and the stones set in the stocks. They burned in a fire, which they had made in the centre of the court, brocade and embroidered shawls for the sake of the gold and silver. China, glass and jade they dashed to pieces in pure wantonness; pictures they ripped, or tossed on the flames, furniture shared the same fate. There are companies which can boast of privates with thousands of pounds worth in their ranks. One man I heard of who complacently offered to lend an officer "whatever sum he wanted if he wished to buy over the Captain". Others have remitted large sums to their friends. Ere this letter reached England, many a diamond, emerald and delicate pearl will have told its tale in a very quiet pleasant way, of the storm and the sack of Kaiserbagh.' The revolt in Lucknow, the capital of Awadh, came to an end under such scenes of plunder.

The place where General Neill of the Madras Fusiliers was killed near Khas Bazaar. Shot through the head, he was killed in September 1857.

Chattar Manzil palace wall and the King's boat in the shape of a fish.

East Gate from the Garden, Kaiser Bagh Lucknow. By March 1858 Sir Colin Campbell had captured the 'symbolic heart of Lucknow', the Kaiser Bagh Palace. The palace was looted and the royal treasures destroyed or stolen.

ABOVE: The *Times* London correspondent, William Howard Russell, looking on at the sacking of Kaiser Bagh after the capture of Lucknow on 16 March 1858.
BELOW: The Stone Bridge on Gomti. Of the two fixed bridges on the river, this bridge was captured by Sir James Outram advancing towards the Badshah Bagh Palace.

Lord Canning, the Governor General of India during the revolt of 1857.

A rebel from Lucknow, Durzee Singh.

UPRISING IN KANPUR

An artist's rendition of massacre at Kanpur.

“THE REVOLT IN KANPUR BEGAN ON THE NIGHT OF 4 JUNE WITH THE FIRING OF GUNS”

The mutiny in Kanpur began on the night of 4 June with the firing of guns and the extensive destruction of British property. But disaffection among the sepoys of Kanpur had been evident from the beginning of May. The first news of disaffection among the sepoys of the Bengal Army reached Kanpur sometime in April 1857 when sepoys of the disbanded 19th Native Infantry reached Kanpur and announced, 'We shall quarrel with the government presently; for new cartridges prepared with cows' and pigs' fat are going to be served out, and the sepoys refuse to receive them.' As the news of the Meerut outbreak reached Kanpur, troops there began to show their hostility to the British. In the bazaar a sergeant's wife was told by a sepoy, 'You will none of you come here much oftener, you will not be alive another week.' On 2 June, one Englishman fired upon a sepoy; at his trial he was acquitted and the sepoys were told that the man had been intoxicated and his musket had gone off by mistake. The sepoys had retorted that possibly their muskets would also go off by mistake. In the sepoy lines *panchayats* were held every night. Immediately after the mutiny, the sepoys went to Kalyanpur where they persuaded the Nana Sahib to join the rebellion and to lead it. The Nana returned to Kanpur with the troops on 7 June and announced to General Wheeler, who had withdrawn with his garrison and the European population into the entrenchment, that he intended to declare war. Thus commenced the siege of the entrenchment which continued till 25 June when the rebels offered the British safe passage by boats to Allahabad.

When Havelock arrived in Allahabad on 30 June, he heard about General Wheeler's surrender. Neill did not believe the report. Havelock first marched to Fatehpur and recovered it from the rebels around 8 July. He could now proceed to Kanpur. But on 15 July, he encountered the rebels at Aong. It was a decisive battle and the defeat of the rebel army set the stage for the attack on Kanpur. He crossed the river Pandu immediately after the battle at Aong. The river was swollen but the bridge, much to the surprise of Havelock, was intact. Havelock occupied the bridge, but only after a fierce battle. Nana's last stand outside Kanpur ended in defeat and Havelock entered Kanpur on 17 July. After the defeat on the banks of Pandu, the rebels retreated into Kanpur, but they were no match for Havelock's troops. But before Havelock made his victorious entry into Kanpur, the rebels decided to kill the survivors, mostly women and children, of the Satichaura Ghat massacre who had been kept as prisoners at the Bibighur. A personal servant of the Nana, called Begum, brought orders from the Nana to the sepoys that the captive women and children should be killed. The sepoys refused to obey and perfunctorily fired a few volleys aimed at the ceiling. When the sepoys refused, four and five professional executioners were sent in armed with swords and long knives. They cut up the prisoners. The bodies – it was said that not all were dead – were thrown into a well. The Nana had left Kanpur for Bithur either immediately after or before the Bibighur killings. He evacuated Bithur under cover of night the day after Havelock entered Kanpur. He staged a suicide by drowning in the Ganges but actually crossed over to Awadh. Thus when Havelock entered Kanpur, he discovered that there was no garrison to relieve. On 19 July British forces under Major Stephenson destroyed the palace in Bithur. Havelock left immediately for Lucknow on 25 July, leaving Neill in charge of operations. The sight of the Bibighur, the well and reports of the Satichaura Ghat massacre had enraged Neill and the British troops. Neill gave orders that those implicated in the rebellion – in his case it meant all Indians, unless proved otherwise – were to be sentenced to death, but before their execution they would have to clean up a portion of the blood on the walls of the Bibighur. They had to do this by licking off the blood. Neill also ordered that after the hangings 'all the Brahmins will be buried and all the Mahomedans burned.'

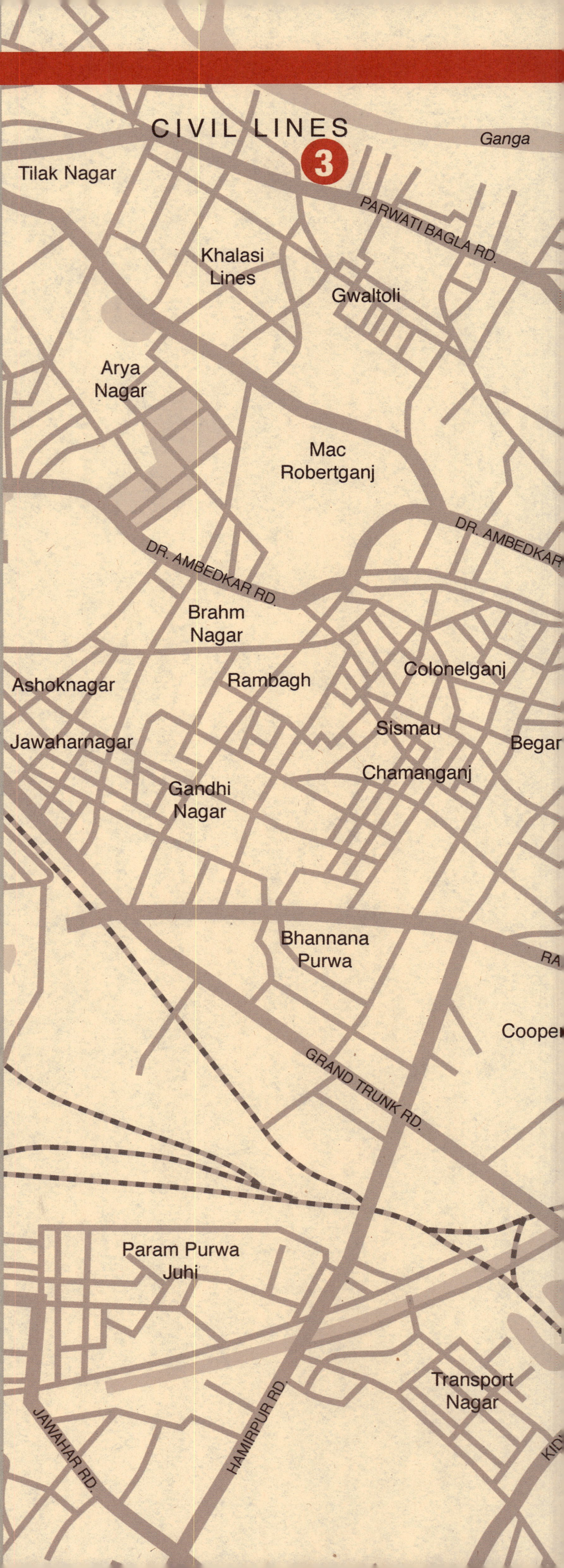

AREAS OF DISTURBANCE
1 Satichaura Ghat
2 Bibighur
3 Civil Lines
4 Cantonment
Parmat
Green Park
Kotwali
Bibighur
Ganga
LUCKNOW RD.
Mulganj
Patkapur
Lalmourbagh
Hatia
Naughara
TAGORE RD.
Collectorganj
Sadr Bazar
Satichaura Ghat
CANTONMENT AREA
MAHATMA GANDHI RD.
Faithfulganj
il Bazar
Mirpur
CAMBRIDGE RD.
CHAKERI RD.
Purwa

General Wheeler's entrenchment, 1858: At the time of rebellion by the sepoys in Kanpur, General Wheeler decided to take refuge in the south of the city, in an entrenchment composed of two barracks surrounded by a mud wall.

What came to be called Wheeler's entrenchment was nothing more than some barracks in the area of the cantonment. The longest of these had a thatched roof and was about 400 feet long and 50 feet wide. Another barrack had a proper roof, but was smaller (40 feet wide and 200 feet wide). Wheeler saw the entrenchment as 'a place of refuge', but it became the 'fort of despair'. For nearly three weeks, this became the home for the Britons in Kanpur. They were surrounded on all sides by rebels who shelled them intermittently. There was also the intense heat of June which the refugees in the entrenchment had to suffer. There was a shortage of water and food. There was one well and those who attempted to draw water became the target of sepoy sharp-shooters. A week into the siege, the thatched roof caught fire from a shell. This fire also burnt all the medical stores. Women and children were left without a roof over their heads and the wounded without any relief. Under these conditions, life continued as did the defence of the entrenchment. The suffering and bravery of those besieged in Kanpur has become the stuff of British heroism. There was general relief when the Nana offered terms of surrender. Little did the rebels guess what fate awaited them when they were about to begin their journey by boat from Satichaura Ghat.

General Wheeler's entrenchment: Nana Sahib's forces attacked the British entrenchment on 6 June 1857. The British were not adequately prepared for the attack, but managed to defend themselves for a long time.

ABOVE: An artist's rendition of massacre at Satichaura Ghat.
BELOW: An artist's rendition of Miss Wheeler defending herself against the sepoys at Kanpur.

Jwala Prasad, one of the loyal followers of Nana Sahib.

ABOVE: Part of General Wheeler's entrenched barrack.
BELOW: Bibighur or Nana Sahib's slaughterhouse: The surviving British women and children from Satichaura Ghat massacre were confined here for a few months before they too were killed brutally and the dead bodies thrown into a well. This incident led to an indiscriminate violence and killings by the British forces.

Nana Sahib of Bithur

According to historians and popular legend, Nana Sahib was never captured by the British, but there were around ten different people at different places claiming to be Nana Sahib. This picture from Public Record Office, Kew, London show the imprisoned Nana Sahib.

Through his adoption, Nana Sahib was heir-presumptive to the throne of Peshwa, and was eligible for an annual pension of £80,000 from the East India Company. However, after the death of Baji Rao II, the Company stopped the pension on the grounds that Nana Sahib was not a natural born heir. This offended Nana Sahib, and he sent his envoy (Azimullah Khan) to England in 1853 to plead his case with the British Government. However, Azimullah Khan was unable to convince the British to resume the pension.

This made him hostile towards the British rulers. During the uprising in 1857, he assumed leadership of the rebels in Kanpur and after seizing Kanpur, which had a small British garrison, commanded by General Wheeler, Nana Sahib proclaimed himself the Peshwa and called for the total extermination of the British power in India. After the Satichaura Ghat massacre and Bibighur massacre, which are considered to be the most violent attacks on the British soldiers and civilians, and which in turn led to an equally violent attack on the Indian sepoys as well as the native villagers, Nana Sahib disappeared from Kanpur after the British Army led by General Havelock recaptured it.

In September 1857, he was reported to have fallen to malarious fever; however, it is not proved. By 1859, Nana Sahib was reported to have fled to Nepal. In February 1860, the British were informed that Nana Sahib's wives had taken refuge in Nepal. Nana Sahib's ultimate fate was never known. Up until 1888 there were rumours and reports that he had been captured and a number of individuals turned themselves in to the British claiming to be the aged Nana. As the majority of these reports turned out to be untrue further attempts at apprehending him were abandoned.

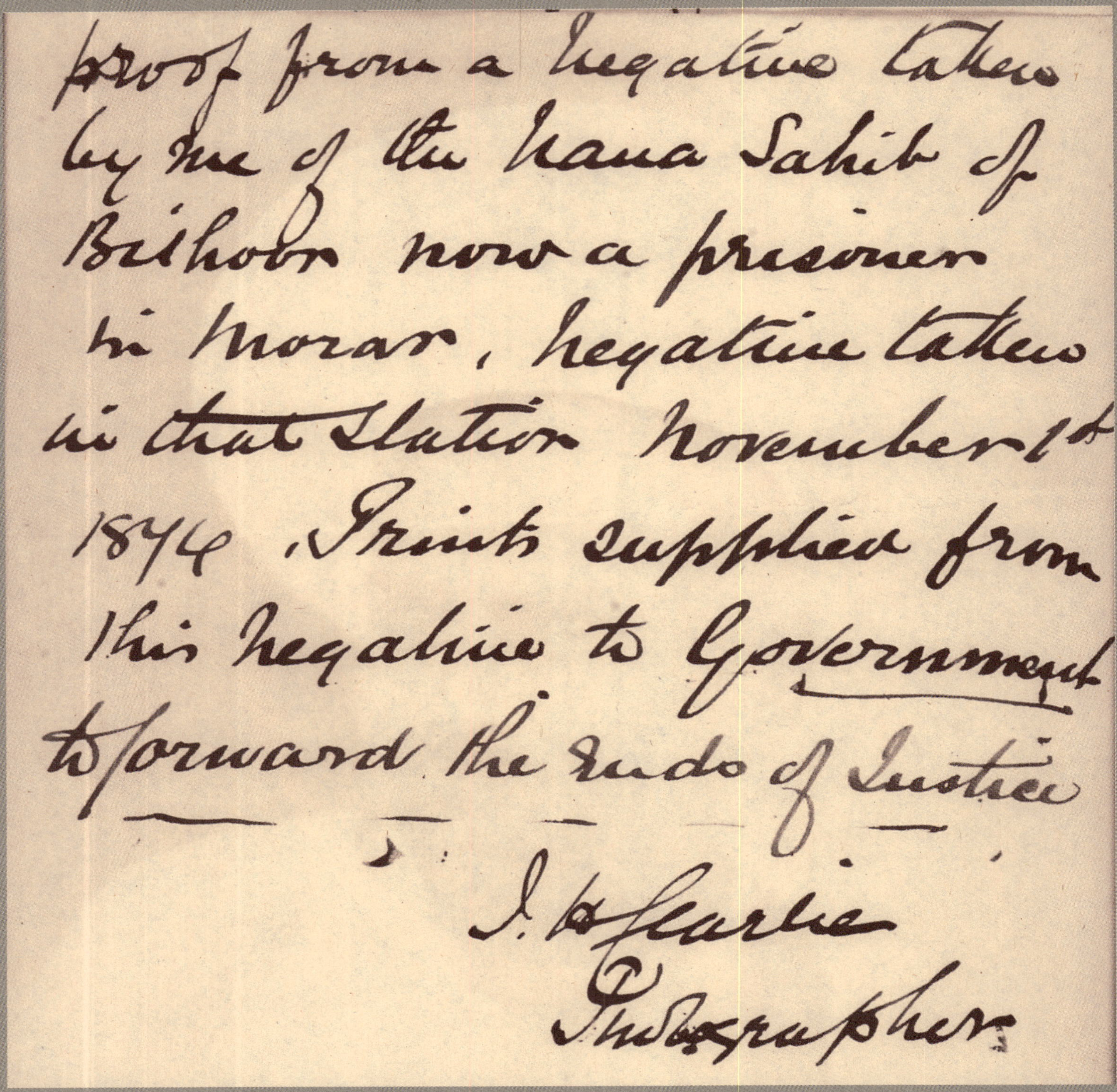

proof from a Negative taken by me of the Nana Sahib of Bithoor now a prisoner in Morar, Negative taken in that Station November 1st 1874. Prints supplied from this Negative to Government to forward the ends of Justice

J. H. Clarke
Photographer

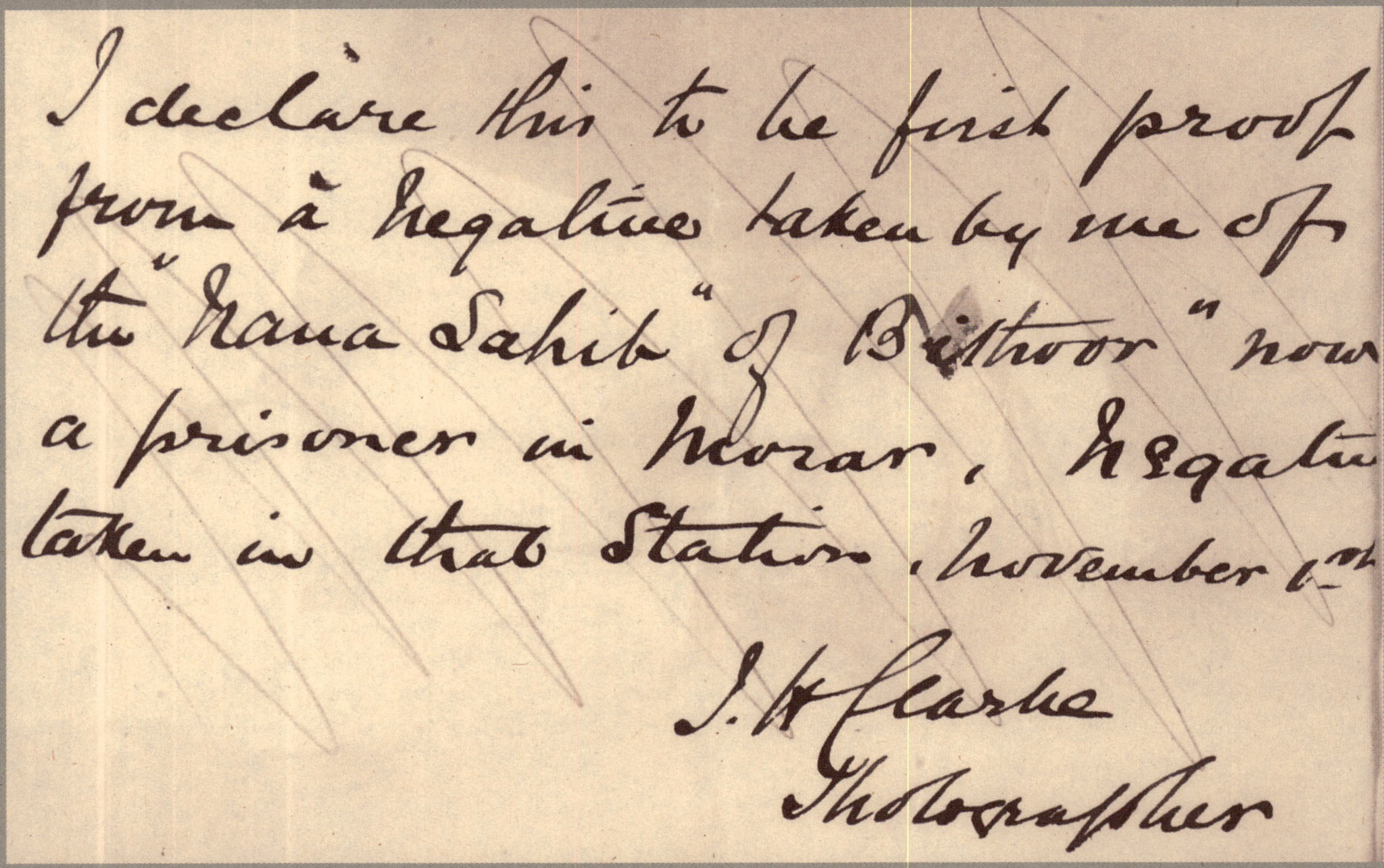

I declare this to be first proof from a Negative taken by me of the "Nana Sahib" of "Bithoor" now a prisoner in Morar, Negative taken in that Station. November 1st

J. H. Clarke
Photographer

Affidavit from the Record Office showing that Nana Sahib of Bithur was imprisoned in Morar.

Another face of Nana Sahib

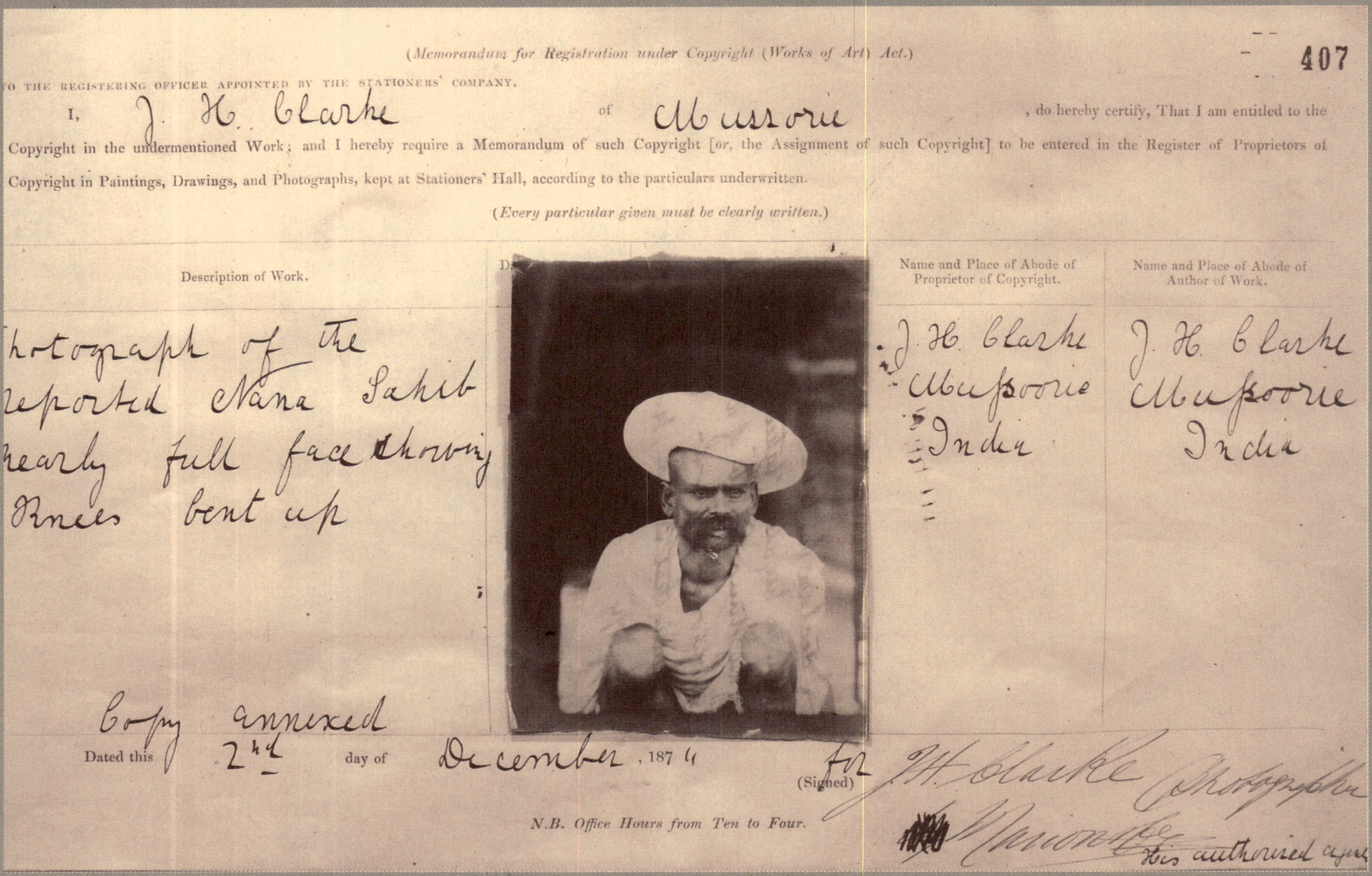

(Memorandum for Registration under Copyright (Works of Art) Act.) 407

TO THE REGISTERING OFFICER APPOINTED BY THE STATIONERS' COMPANY.

I, J. H. Clarke of Mussoorie, do hereby certify, That I am entitled to the Copyright in the undermentioned Work; and I hereby require a Memorandum of such Copyright [or, the Assignment of such Copyright] to be entered in the Register of Proprietors of Copyright in Paintings, Drawings, and Photographs, kept at Stationers' Hall, according to the particulars underwritten.

(Every particular given must be clearly written.)

Description of Work.		Name and Place of Abode of Proprietor of Copyright.	Name and Place of Abode of Author of Work.
Photograph of the reported Nana Sahib nearly full face showing knees bent up		J. H. Clarke Mussoorie India	J. H. Clarke Mussoorie India

Copy annexed

Dated this 2nd day of December, 1874

(Signed) for J. H. Clarke (Photographer)

N.B. Office Hours from Ten to Four.

Manion & Co. His authorised agent

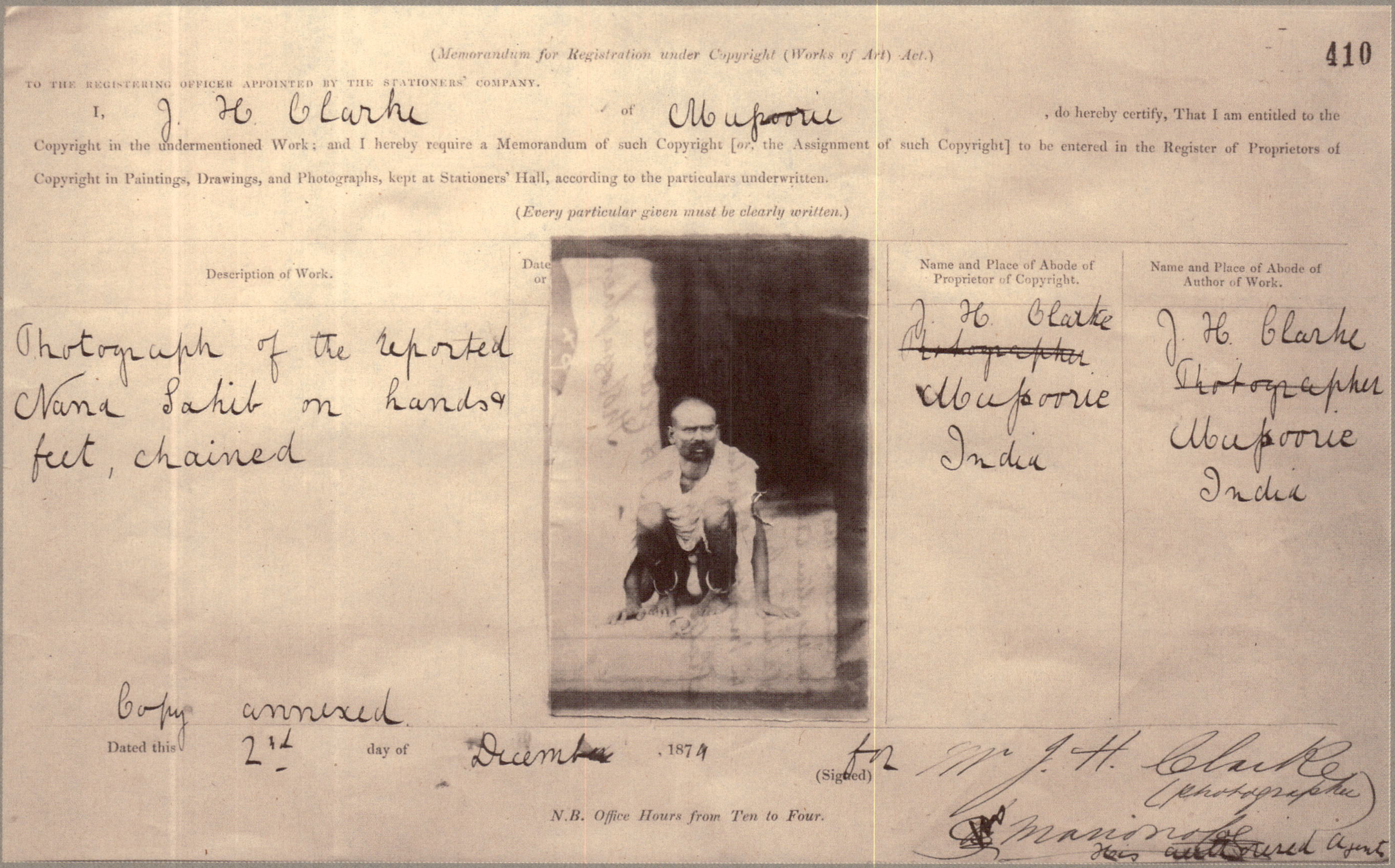

(Memorandum for Registration under Copyright (Works of Art) Act.) 410

TO THE REGISTERING OFFICER APPOINTED BY THE STATIONERS' COMPANY.

I, J. H Clarke of Mussoorie, do hereby certify, That I am entitled to the Copyright in the undermentioned Work; and I hereby require a Memorandum of such Copyright [or, the Assignment of such Copyright] to be entered in the Register of Proprietors of Copyright in Paintings, Drawings, and Photographs, kept at Stationers' Hall, according to the particulars underwritten.

(Every particular given must be clearly written.)

Description of Work.	Date or	Name and Place of Abode of Proprietor of Copyright.	Name and Place of Abode of Author of Work.
Photograph of the reported Nana Sahib on hands & feet, chained		J. H. Clarke ~~Photographer~~ Mussoorie India	J. H. Clarke ~~Photographer~~ Mussoorie India

Copy annexed

Dated this 2nd day of December, 1874

(Signed) for Mr J. H. Clarke (Photographer)

N.B. Office Hours from Ten to Four.

Manion & Co. His authorised Agent

Affidavit submitted by J.H. Clarke on 2 December 1874, of the reported Nana Sahib with his hands and feet chained.

Another face of Nana Sahib

UPRISING IN JHANSI

Field Marshal Hugh Henry Rose (sitting second from right), 1st Baron Strathnairn. In May 1857 he took command of the forces in Central India, and after fierce battles at Mhow, Madanpur and Chanderi, arrived at Jhansi on 10 March 1858 and during the siege defeated a relieving force under Tantia Topi at the Betwa on 1 April 1858.

> "THE OTHER THING THAT STILL REMAINS UNCLEAR IS THE RANI OF JHANSI'S KNOWLEDGE OF AND INVOLVEMENT IN THE MASSACRE."

Jhansi was a small Maratha principality in Bundelkhand which Lord Dalhousie annexed in March 1854. The news of the outbreak in Meerut and the fall of Delhi reached Jhansi in May. In June the 21st Native Infantry stationed in Jhansi received the news that all the sepoys of the Bengal Army had mutinied but the regiment in Jhansi had not. Thus the men of that regiment had lost their faith. This incited the sepoys who mutinied on 5 June. The British took refuge in the fort. The mutineers blockaded the fort, and it soon became a matter of time when the refugees in the fort would run out of provisions. On the 8th the British were forced to come out of the fort. It has never been clear whether the rebels had promised the British safe conduct. As soon as they came out of the fort, every single Briton, including women and children, were killed. The dead bodies remained in the open for three days in Jokhan Bagh where the massacre took place, and then they were buried in a common pit. The other thing that still remains unclear is the Rani of Jhansi's knowledge of and involvement in the massacre. The British liked to believe that she was implicated.

AREA OF DISTURBANCE

1 Fort

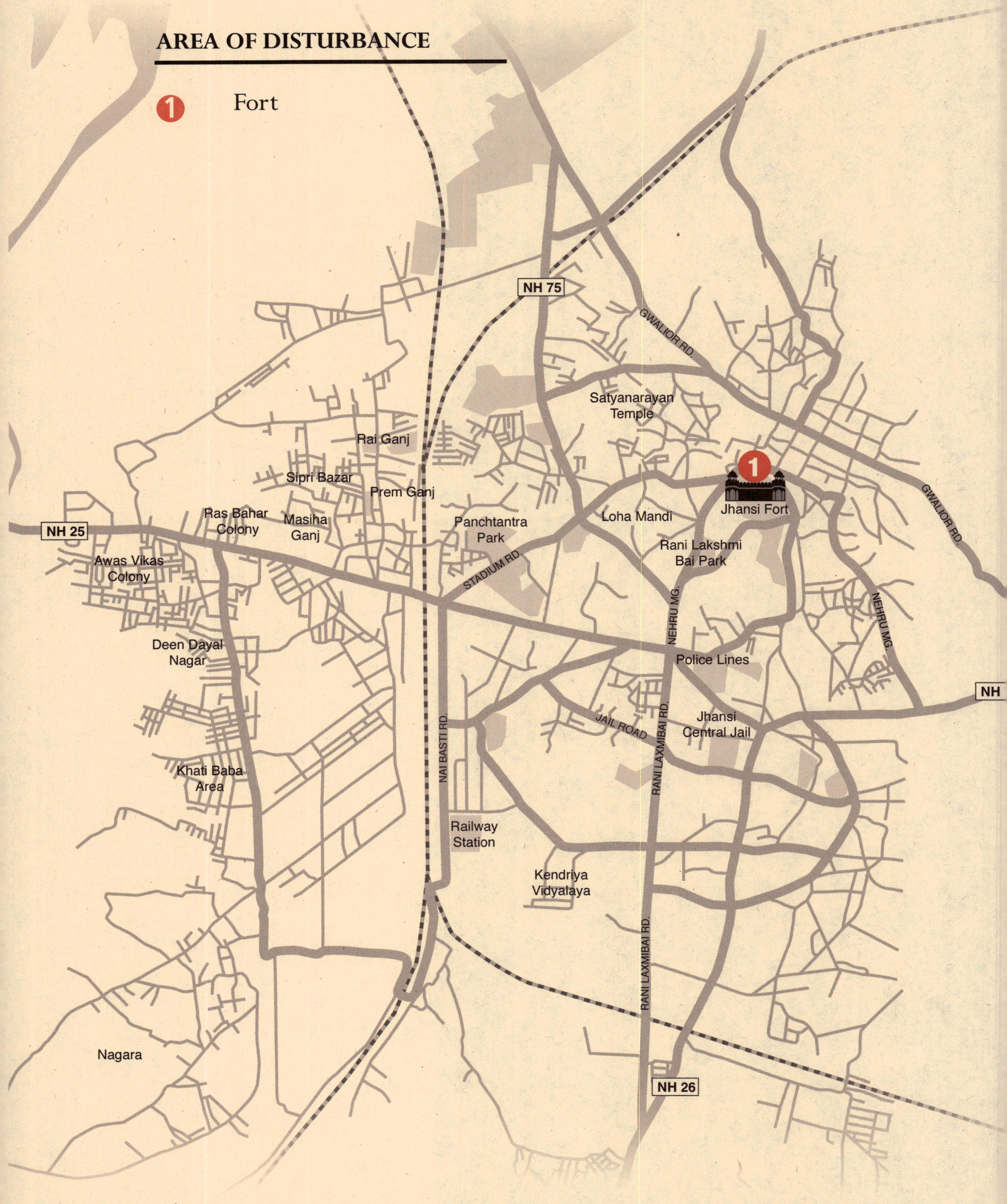

The British force under Hugh Rose arrived in Jhansi to relieve it on 21 March 1858. The siege began the next day. Four days later, the cannonading of the ramparts began. The fire was returned by the rebels, and the British noticed that even women were at work trying to repair damages. The Rani herself supervised the work. The fort proved to be exceptionally strong. In the meantime on the 31st, Tantia Topi arrived with an army of 20,000 men. Rose had thus to devote his attention to the rebel army outside the fort. He divided his forces: one to continue to the siege and the other to fight Tantia Topi. The latter was defeated in a hard-fought battle. Rose was now free to concentrate on Jhansi. The rebels were, however, not demoralized by the defeat of Tantia Topi. When Rose opened his assault on the fort, he met with a fierce resistance. The rebels fired at them but also hurled all manner of things at them – earthen pots filled with powder, logs of wood, etc. The fort was finally breached but this was only the beginning of the reconquest of Jhansi. Now the resistance to the British occurred in every street, in every house and in every room. This was on 3 April. The palace was taken through this process of bayonet-to-bayonet, hand-to-hand fighting. But the fighting in the streets continued till the next day. Once the British was certain they were the victors, they proceeded to sack the city and destroyed the famous library of Sanskrit manuscripts. Every Indian was treated as an enemy and dealt with ruthlessly. To escape the avenging army, men who could not escape threw their women and babies down wells and then jumped in themselves. But the British missed their principal target, Lakshmibai, the Rani of Jhansi. The Rani left Jhansi at night disguised as a man and took her adopted son with her. She had as escort a group of faithful Afghans. Confronted by a piquet, the group scattered and could not reunite. The rani and a handful of troopers rode towards Kalpi and covered twenty-one miles in one night. When her flight was discovered in Jhansi by the British, a pursuit was ordered. The Rani's troopers fought back the pursuers, and she rode on to fight another day.

> **“THE NEWS OF THE OUTBREAK IN MEERUT AND THE FALL OF DELHI REACHED JHANSI IN MAY.”**

NOTES

1. Christopher Hibbert, *The Great Mutiny: India, 1857* (Harmondsworth, 1980) recreates (pp. 68-72) the drama of the Mangal Pandey episode. I follow Hibbert's narrative.
2. See for example Vivian Majendie, *Up Among the Pandies: A Year's Service in India* (London, 1859).
3. Lawrence to Canning, 9 May 1857: quoted in H.B. Edwardes and M. Merivale, *Life of Sir Henry Lawrence*, 2 vols (London, 1872), ii, p.322.
4. My analysis of rumours is indebted to Guha's discussion of the subject in *Elementary Aspects of Peasant Insurgency in Colonial India* (Delhi, 1983), pp.251-68. All quotations from Guha in the above two paragraphs will be found in these pages.
5. G.F. Harvey, commissioner Agra division, 'Narrative of Events attending to the Outbreak of Disturbances and the Restoration of Authority in the Agra Division in 1857-58': *FSUP*, I, p.392.
6. G. Hutchinson, *Narrative of the Mutinies in Oude* (London, 1859): quoted in Kaye: I, p.637.
7. W. Edwards, *Personal Adventures during the Indian Rebellion in Rohilcund, Futtehghur and Oude* (London, 1858), pp.15-16.
8. R.H.W. Dunlop, *Service and Adventure with the Khakee Ressallah* (London, 1858), p.26.
9. J.W. Sherer, *Daily Life During the Indian Mutiny* (London, 1898), pp.7-8.
10. C.T. Metcalfe, *Two Native Narratives of the Mutiny in Delhi* (London, 1898), p.69.
11. Readers familiar with the historiography of the English Revolution in the seventeenth century will recognize that I am following the framework of Lawrence Stone in *The Causes of the English Revolution* (London, 1972).
12. See H. Sharp, *Selections from Educational Records, 1781-1839* (Calcutta, 1920), pp.81-86.
13. Ibid., p.22.
14. Ibid., pp.99-101.
15. For Ram Mohun see V.C. Joshi (ed.) *Rammohun Roy and the Process of Modernization in India* (Delhi, 1974); and for Vidyasagar, see Asok Sen, *Iswarchandra Vidyasagar and his Elusive Milestones* (Calcutta, 1977).
16. R. Guha, *An Indian Historiography of India: A Nineteenth Century Agenda and its Implications* (Calcutta, 1988), p.4.
17. Sleeman to Colvin, 28 Dec. 1853: W.H. Sleeman, *A Journey Through the Kingdom of Oude in 1849-50*, 2 vols (London, 1858), ii, p.415.
18. Ibid., pp.66-67.
19. W. Crooke, 'Songs about the King of Oude', No. 5, verse 15: *The Indian Antiquary*, vol. XL, 1911, pp.61-67.
20. For a clear formulation of Dalhousie's views and policies and the debates that ensued within British administration, see Kaye, *Sepoy War*, i, ch.2.
21. Dalhousie to G.C. Bart, 2 May 1855: J.G.A. Baird (ed.) *Private Letters of the Marquess of Dalhousie* (London, 1910), p.344.
22. Letter dated 30 July to G.C. Bart: ibid., p.169.
23. ibid.
24. The only study of this mutiny is P.K. Bandopadhyay, *Tulsi Leaves and the Ganges Water: The Slogan of the First Sepoy Mutiny in Barrackpore* (Kolkata, 2003).
25. Quoted in Hibbert, *The Great Mutiny*, p.56.
26. The firearms used by the British in India in the nineteenth century are discussed in Palmer, *Mutiny Outbreak in Meerut*, pp. 101ff and in David, *Mutiny*, p.52.
27. See David, *Mutiny*, p.53.
28. Forrest, *Selections*, i, pp.7-9.
29. For an account of the Berhampore incident see Palmer, *Mutiny Outbreak in Meerut*, pp.23-25.
30. Quoted in Hibbert, *Great Mutiny*, p.73.
31. My account of the Meerut mutiny is taken from J.A.B. Palmer, *The Mutiny Outbreak at Meerut in 1857* (Cambridge, 1966). Unless otherwise mentioned all facts and quotations are taken from Palmer's book, page numbers are indicated in brackets in the text.
32. Hugh Gough, *Old Memories* (Edinburgh, 1897): cited in Hibbert, *Great Mutiny*, p.85.
33. Quoted in Saul, *Indian Mutiny*, p.104.
34. Lawrence to Edmonstone, 29 May 1857: Inclosure 135 in No 19. Appendix Papers Relative to the Mutinies in the East Indies, p.341, *Papers Relating to Indian Mutinies*, 3 vols (London, 1857).
35. National Archives of India (NAI): Foreign Dept., Secret Consultations, 18 Dec., 1857, No 565: Henry Lawrence to Canning, 3 May 1857.
36. For troops coming from Benares to Lucknow see *FSUP*, ii, p.14; for Faizabad see NAI: Foreign Dept., Secret Consulations, 25 September, 1857: No 398: Bradford to Edmonstone, 2 July 1857; for Salon see Barrow's narrative in G. Hutchinson, *Narrative of the Mutinies in Oude* (London, 1859), pp.127ff.
37. W. Edwards, *Personal Adventures during the Indian Rebellion in Rohilcund, Futtehghur and Oude* (1858; repr., Allahabad, 1974), p.65.
38. R.H.W. Dunlop, *Service and Adventure with the khakee ressalah or Meerut Volunteer Force during the Mutinies of 1857-58* (1858; repr. Allahabad, 1974), pp.153-54.
39. Hearsey's account in Hutchinson, *Narrative*, p.97.
40. Ball, pp.299-300.
41. *Narrative of Events Attending the Outbreak of Disturbances and the Restoration of Authority* (Calcutta, 1858), Meerut, p.253, para 192.
42. Cited in Guha, *Elementary Aspects*, p.141.
43. Quoted in Kaye, ii, p.258.
44. Dunlop, *Service and Adventure*, p.36.
45. *Narrative of Events*, Meerut, p.252, para 172.
46. For this analysis I have depended on my own work. See *Spectre of Violence*, pp.23-46.
47. The absence of rape is analysed in the next chapter.
48. NAI: Foreign Dept., Secret Consultations, 26 June 1857, Nos 52-4: Gubbins to Couper, 27 May 1857.
49. See Seema Alavi, *The Sepoys and the Company: Tradition and Transition in Northern India, 1770-1830* (Delhi, 1995), ch. 2.

50. The data is summarized in Mukherjee (1984) and the policy for recruitment from the region analysed in Alavi (1995).
51. M. Gubbins, *An Account of the Mutinies in Oude and the Seige of the Lucknow Residency* (London, 1858), p.118.
52. *Narrative of Events attending the outbreak of disturbances and the restoration of authority* (Calcutta, 1858), Meerut, p.251, para 165.
53. G. Williams, 'Review of the Evidence taken at Cawnpore regarding the revolt at that station in June and July 1857' in *Narrative of the Events in the NWP in 1857-58* (Calcutta, n.d.).
54. 'Synopsis of the evidence of the Cawnpore Mutiny' in *Narrative of Events in NWP*.
55. See depositions of Gobind Singh, Sheikh Elahee Buksh and Ghouse Mohomed and of the drummer John Fitchett in *Depositions taken at Cawnpore under the direction of Lieutenant Colonel G.W. Williams* printed with *Narrative of Events in NWP*.
56. Narrative of Ganga Singh: India Office Library and Records, Board's Collection No 195718.
57. *Narrative of Events*, Meerut, p.251, para 165.
57a. India Office Library and Records (IOLR), Board's Collection, No 191546: Revolt of the Native Army: Measures Adopted for the Punishment of Mutineers, Deserters and Rebels, dated 11 December 1857.
57b. Roberts, *Letters Written during the Indian Mutiny* (London, 1924), p.119.
58. This chronology is spelt out in Mukherjee, *Awadh in Revolt*, ch. 4.
59. Gubbins, *Mutinies*, pp.189-90.
60. See Mukherjee, *Awadh in Revolt*, p.84.
61. Telegram from Lt.Col. Tytler to the C-in-C, 6 August 1857: cited in ibid., p.86.
62. Officer commanding at Allahabad to C-in-C, 18 August 1857: Inclosure 97 in No 2 *Further Papers* (No 4), p.101, *Papers Relating to Indian Mutinies*, 3 vols (at the Indian Institute Library, Oxford).
63. Letter to Outram (signature illegible), 30 August 1857: Mutiny Papers of Outram, Havelock and Campbell: Eur.Mss. C124 at the India Office Library and Records, London.
64. Charles Ball, *The History of the Indian Mutiny*, 2 vols (London, n.d.) ii, p.44.
65. Couper to Edmonstone, 21 November 1857: Foreign Secret Consultations, 29 January 1858, Cons. No 341 (National Archives of India, New Delhi).
66. Carnegy's intelligence, For. Dept., Secret Branch, 26 February, 1858, Cons. No 228 (News of 4 Oct 1857).
67. Ibid.,
68. Ibid., news of 23 October 1857.
69. Ibid., news of 15 December 1857. The newsletter containing these figures was dated 15 December but it made clear that it was at least a fortnight old. I think that it is safe to assume that the numbers pertain to Campbell's relief since that was the period when the fighting was at its heaviest.
70. Ibid., news of 25 November 1857.
71. Ibid., Cons. No 227 news of 4 January 1857. Details of efforts to fortify the city are in Mukherjee, *Awadh in Revolt*, p.96.
72. Couper to Edmonstone, 15 December1857: For. Dept. Secret Cons., 26 March 1858, Cons. 63.
73. Couper to Edmonstone, 9 December 1857: For. Dept. Secret Cons. 29 January 1858, No. 346.
74. For details see Mukherjee, *Awadh in Revolt*, pp.98-99.
75. Carnegy's intelligence, For. Dept., Secret Branch, 26 February 1858, Cons No 228 (news of 16 Nov. 1857) and No 227 (news of 1 January 1858).
76. Letter from the secretary to the government, Central Provinces, to the secretary to the government of India, 15 October 1857: Inclosure in No 7, *Further Papers* (No 7), p.71, *Papers Relating to Indian Mutinies*.
77. Carnegy's intelligence, For. Dept., Secret Branch, 26 February, 1858, No 228 (news of 20 November 1857).
78. Extracts of intelligence from Carnegy, 13 October 1857: *Further Papers* (No 7), p.74, *Papers Re Indian Mutinies*.
79. M. Maclagan, *Clemency Canning* (London, 1962) pp.174-75 argues that this was a military blunder on the part of the British. For a contrary view that this escape of the rebels was possible because the British army immediately after the fall of Lucknow was rendered inactive by the greed for looting and for a few days had ceased to be an army at all, see K. Marx and F. Engels, *The First War of Indian Independence* (Moscow, n.d.) pp.136-37 and 152.
80. W.H. Russell, *My Indian Mutiny Diary* edited by M. Edwardes (London, 1957) p.119.
81. Quoted in ibid., p.73.
82. Forsyth to Edmonstone, 5 June 1858., For. Dept., Secret Cons., 30 July 1858, Cons. No 63.
83. For details see Mukherjee, *Awadh in Revolt*, pp. 111-12.
84. Ibid.
85. Ibid., pp.116-17.
86. Ibid., pp.118-120.
87. For details, ibid., pp. 121ff.
88. Ibid., pp.127-34.
89. Collection to Political Despatches 33 Part 2, Collection No 21 (India Office Library and Records, London).
90. List of Arms surrendered 16 December 1858: For. Dept. Political Cons. 31 December 1858, Cons. No 244.
91. Capt. Thomas to Commissioner of Ordnance, 1 June 1858, Board of Revenue, Oudh General (UP State Archives, Lucknow) File No 754.
92. See Mukherjee, *Awadh in Revolt*, p.166.
93. The following account of the civil rebellion in Bundelkhand is based on Tapti Roy, *The Politics of a Popular Uprising: Bundelkhand in 1857* (New Delhi, 1994). I have omitted references to original sources and referred to Roy's monograph.
94. See Roy, pp.218-19.
95. Roy, pp. 221ff; the quotation is from p.225.

96. Roy, p.229.
97. Roy, pp.158-60.
98. Roy, pp.162-63.
99. Roy, pp.166-95.
100. Roy, pp.103-05.
101. Roy, pp.105-07.
102. Roy, pp.107-08.
103. Roy, p.108.
104. Roy, pp.109-10.
105. Roy, pp.113-14.
106. Roy, pp.110-12.
107. Roy, p. 113.
108. This last phase is described in Roy, pp.117-33.
109. IOLR, Board's Collection, No 191547: Revolt of the Native Army: Measures Adopted for the Punishment of Mutineers, Deserters and Rebels, dated 24 December 1857.
110. *Daily News*, 25 August 1857, letter dated 23 June 1857: cited in R.M. Martin, *Our Indian Empire*, 2 vols (London, n.d.), ii, p.302.
111. IOLR: Board's Collection 191546.
112. Proclamation enclosed with translation of a pamphlet entited *Fateh Islam*: *FSUP*, ii, pp.160-62.
113. Proclamation issued under the seal of Birjis Qadr: For. Dept., Secret Cons., 25 June 1858, Cons No 69.
114. NAI: Proclamation issued by Prince Mirza Mahomed Feroze Shah on 17 February 1858: For. Dept. Secret Cons. Nos. 121-22.
115. This version is available in *FSUP*, i, pp. 459-63.
116. C. Ball, *History of the Indian Mutiny*, 2 vols (London, n.d.), ii, p.242.
117. Abstract translation of an Arzi from the rebel camp on the part of all the rebel officers, sepoys to Maharaja Jang Bahadur, no date: For. Dept., Political Cons., 13 May 1859, Cons. No 326: *FSUP*, ii, pp.603-05.
118. The full text of this Proclamation, known as the Azamgarh Proclamation and issued on 25 August 1857 in the name of Bahadur Shah is available in Ball, *The Mutiny*, ii, pp.630-32 and in *FSUP*, I, pp. 453-58.
119. This discussion on rape is taken from Mukherjee (1984), pp.162-65, all quotations are taken from there.
120. Proclamation issued by the Begum in the name of Birjis Qadr: For. Dept., Political Cons. 17 December 1858, Cons No 251.
121. Ibid.
122. See Eric Stokes, *The Peasant and the Raj: Studies in Agrarian Society and Peasant Rebellion in Colonial India* (Cambridge, 1978), pp.133 and 135.
123. Quoted in Mukherjee (1984), p.169n139.
124. Stokes, *Peasant and the Raj*, p.132.
125. G.B. Malleson, *History of the Indian Mutiny, 1857-58*, 3 vols (London, 2nd ed., 1878), i, pp.407-08n.
126. K.K. Datta, *Biography of Kunwar Singh and Amar Singh* (Patna, 1957).
127. C.A. Bayly, *Information and Empire: Intelligence-Gathering and Social Communication in India, 1780-1870* (Cambridge, 1996), pp.320-24.
128. Ibid.
129. Forsyth to Edmonstone, 2 October 1858: For. Dept., Political Cons., 15 October 1858, Cons. No 279.
130. See proclamation issued by Feroze Shah.
131. Ball, *The Mutiny*, ii, p.550.

BIBLIOGRAPHY

ARCHIVAL SOURCES

BRITISH LIBRARY: INDIA OFFICE RECORDS

Home Miscellaneous Series

Board's Collection

North Western Provinces Proceedings (Political)

Collection to Political Despatches

NATIONAL ARCHIVES OF INDIA, NEW DELHI

Foreign Department, Secret Consulations.

Foreign Department, Political Consulations.

Foreign Department, Secret Proceedings.

Foreign Department, Political Proceedings.

PRINTED SOURCES

Forrest, G.W., *Selections from the Letters, Dispatches and other State Papers preserved in the Military Department of the Government of India, 1857-58*, 4 vols (Calcutta, 1893-1912).

Narrative of Events in the NWP in 1857-58 (Calcutta, n.d.)

Narrative of Events attending the Outbreak of Disturbances and the Restoration of Authority, 2 vols (Calcutta, 1881).

Papers Relating to Indian Mutinies, 3 vols (London, n.d.).

Rizvi, S.A., and Bhargava, M.L., *Freedom Struggle in Uttar Pradesh*, 6 vols (Govt. of UP, Lucknow, 1957).

Sharp, H., *Selections from Educational Records* (Calcutta, 1920).

BOOKS AND ARTICLES

Alavi, Seema, *The Sepoys and the Company: Tradition and Transition in Northern India, 1770-1830* (Delhi, 1995).

Amin, S., "English Domination and Indian Subordination", *Biblio*, July-August, 1997.

Ball, C., *The History of the Indian Mutiny* (London, n.d.).

Bandyopadhyay, P.K., *Tulsi Leaves and the Ganges Water: The Slogan of the First Sepoy Mutiny in Barrackpore 1824* (Calcutta, 2003).

Barat, A., *The Bengal Native Infantry: Its Organization and Discipline, 1796-1852* (Calcutta, 1962).

Bayly, C.A., *Information and Empire: Intelligence Gathering and Social Communication in India, 1780-1870* (Cambridge, 1996).

——. *Origins of Nationality in South Asia: Patriotism and Ethical Government in the Making Of Modern India* (Delhi, 1998).

——. *Rulers, Townsmen and Bazaars: North Indian Society in the Age of British Expansion, 1770-1870* (Cambridge, 1983).

Bhadra, G., "Four Rebels of 1857" in R. Guha (ed.) *Subaltern Studies: Writings on South Asian History and Society*, vol. IV (Delhi, 1986).

Bhatnagar, G.D., "The Annexation of Oudh", *Uttara Bahrati*, vol. III (1956).

Buckler, F.W., "The Political Theory of the Indian Mutiny", *Royal Historical Society Transactions*, Series 4, vol. V, 1932.

Butter, D., *Outline of the Topography and Statistics of the Southern Districts of Oudh* (Calcutta, 1839).

Chattaopadhyaya, H.P., "The Sepoy Army: Its strength, composition and recruitment", *Calcutta Review*, May, June, July, August 1956.

Chaudhuri, S.B., *Civil Rebellion in the Indian Mutinies (1857-59)* (Calcutta, 1957).

——. *English Historical Writings on the Indian Mutiny (1857-59)* (Calcutta, 1979).

——. *Civil Disturbances during British Rule in India* (Calcutta, 1955).

——. *Theories of the Indian Mutiny, 1857-59* (Calcutta, 1965).

Clive, John, *Macaulay: The Shaping of the Historian* (Harvard, 1973).

Crooke, W., "Songs about the King of Oudh", *Indian Antiquary*, vol. XL, 1911.

Dalrymple, W., *The Last Mughal: The Fall of a Dynasty, Delhi, 1857* (Delhi, 2006).

Datta, K.K., *Biography of Kunwar Singh and Amar Singh* (Patna, 1957).

David, Saul, *The Indian Mutiny: 1857*, (Viking, London, 2002).

Dundas Robertson, H., *District Duties during the Revolt in the North West Provinces of India in 1857 with Subsequent Investigations during 1858-59* (London, 1859).

Dunlop, R.H.W., *Service and Adventure with the Khakee Ressalah or Meerut Volunteer Horse, during the Mutinies of 1857-58* (Allahabad, repr., 1974).

Edwards, W., *Personal Adventures during the Indian Rebellion in Rohilcund, Futtehgurh and Oude* (London, 1858; Allahabad repr. 1974).

Edwardes, H.B., and Merivale, H., *Life of Sir Henry Lawrence*, 2 vols (London, 1873).

Forbes-Mitchell, W., *Reminiscences of the Great Mutiny, 1857-59* (London, 1894).

Gopal, S., *Jawaharlal Nehru: A Biography*, vol. I (London, 1975).

Gubbins, M., *An Account of the Mutinies in Oude and the Siege of the Lucknow Residency* (London, 1858).

Guha, Ranajit, *Elementary Aspects of Peasant Insurgency in Colonial India* (Delhi, 1983).

——. "The Prose of Counter Insurgency" in Ranajit Guha (ed.), *Subaltern Studies: Writings on South Asian History and Society*, vol. II (Delhi, 1983).

——. *Dominance without Hegemony: History and Power in Colonial India* (Delhi, 1998).

Gupta, P.C., *Nana Sahib and the Rising in Cawnpore* (Oxford, 1963).

Hibbert, C., *The Great Mutiny: India, 1857* (Harmondsworth, 1978).

Hutchinson, G., *Narrative of the Mutinies in Oudh* (London, 1859).

Joshi, P.C., *Rebellion, 1857: A Symposium* (Delhi, 1957).

Kaye, J.W., *History of the Sepoy War*, 3 vols (London, 1864-1880).

Kopf, D., *British Orientalism and the Bengal Renaissance* (Berkeley, 1969).

Maclagan, M., *Clemency Canning* (London, 1962).

Majumdar, R. C., *The Sepoy Mutiny and the Revolt of 1857*, (Calcutta, 1957).

Malleson, G.B., *A History of the Indian Mutiny* (London, 1878-80).

Martin, R.M., *Our Indian Empire*, 2 vols (London, n.d.).

Marx, K., *The First War of Indian Independence, 1857-58* (Moscow, 1959).

Metcalf, T.R., *The Aftermath of Revolt: India, 1857-1870* (Princeton, 1964).

——. *Land, Landlords and the British Raj: Northern India in the Nineteenth Century* (Berkeley, 1979).

——. "The Oudh Talukdar: From Raja to Landlord" in R.E. Frykenberg (ed.) *Land Control and Social Structure in Indian History* (Wisconsin, 1969).

Metcalfe, C.T., *Two Native Narratives of the Mutiny in Delhi* (London, 1898).

Mitra, R.C., "Education" in N.K. Sinha (ed.) *The History of Bengal (1757-1905)* (Calcutta, 1967).

Mukherjee, R., *Awadh in Revolt, 1857-58: A Study of Popular Resistance*, (Delhi, 1984, repr., 2001).

——. *Spectre of Violence: The 1857 Kanpur Massacres* (Delhi, 1998).

——. *Mangal Pandey: Brave Martyr or Accidental Hero?* (Delhi, 2005).

——. "Trade and Empire in Awadh, 1765-1804", *Past and Present*, No. 94, February 1982.

——. "Satan let loose upon Earth: The Kanpur Massacres in India in the Revolt of 1857", *Past and Present*, No 128, August 1990.

——. "The Azamgarh Proclamation and some questions on the Revolt of 1857 in the North-Western Provinces" in *Essays in Honour of Prof. S.C. Sarkar* (Delhi, 1976).

Palmer, J.A.B., *The Mutiny Outbreak in Meerut in 1857* (CUP, Cambridge, 1966).

Pemble, J., *The Raj, the Indian Mutiny and the Kingdom of Oudh* (Sussex, 1977).

Ray, Tapti, *The Politics of a Popular Uprising: Bundelkhand in 1857* (OUP, Delhi, 1996).

Reeves, Peter, (ed.), *Sleeman in Oudh*, (CUP, Cambridge, 1971).

Rice Holmes, T., *History of the Indian Mutiny* (London, 1904).

Roberts, F., *Letters Written during the Indian Mutiny* (London, 1924).

Russell, W.H., *My Indian Mutiny Diary*, ed., M. Edwards (New York, 1970).

Savarkar, V.D., *The Indian War of Independence, 1857* (London, 1909).

Sen, S.N., *1857* (Publications Division, Delhi, 1957).

Sleeman, W.H., *A Journey Through the Kingdom of Oude*, 2 vols (London, 1858).

Siddiqi, A., *Agrarian Change in a Northern Indian State: Uttar Pradesh, 1818-33* (Oxford, 1973).

Sitaram, *From Sepoy to Subedar*, ed. by James Lunt, translated by Capt. Norgate (London, 1970).

Spear, T.G.P., *Twilight of the Mughals* (Cambridge, 1951).

Stokes, Eric, *The Peasant and the Raj: Studies in Agrarian Society and Peasant Rebellion in Colonial India* (CUP, Cambridge, 1978).

——. *The Peasant Armed: The Indian Rebellion of 1857* (OUP, Bombay, 1986).

——. *English Utilitarians and India* (Oxford, 1959).

——. "North and Central India" in D. Kumar (ed.) *The Cambridge Economic History of India, 1757-1970*, vol. II (Cambridge, 1982; Delhi, repr. 1984).

Taylor, P.J.O., *Companion to the Indian Mutiny of 1857* (OUP, Delhi, 1996).

Thomas, K., *Religion and the Decline of Magic* (Harmondsworth, 1973).

Thornhill, M., *Personal Adventures and Experiences of a Magistrate during the Rise, Progress and Suppression of the Indian Mutiny* (London, 1884).